The Preacher's Struggle and Stamina

The Preacher's Struggle and Stamina

Insight from the Lives of the Apostle Paul and C. H. Spurgeon

including a biography of Spurgeon's life

Volume One

by
Frank R. Shivers

Unless otherwise noted, Scripture quotations are from
The Holy Bible *King James Version*

Library of Congress Cataloging-in-Publication Data

Shivers, Frank R., 1949-
The Preacher's Struggle and Stamina Vol. 1 / Frank Shivers
ISBN 978-1-878127-50-1

Library of Congress Control Number:
2022921475

Cover design by
Tim King

For Information:
Frank Shivers Evangelistic Association
2005 Congress Road
Hopkins, South Carolina 29061
www.frankshivers.com

PRESENTED TO

_____

BY

_____

DATE

_____

"The man who realizes God's presence is by that
invisible companionship rendered invincible."[1]
~ C. H. Spurgeon

"Let no man who looks for ease of mind and seeks quietude of life enter the ministry; if he does so, he will flee from it in disgust."[2] ~ C. H. Spurgeon

To

Laneir Singleton

Laneir (Leroy) was one of the first students I met during freshman orientation in 1967 at the Baptist College at Charleston, Charleston, South Carolina (now CSU). Little did we realize that meeting would initiate a lifetime of unbroken friendship for 57 years and counting. As mere teenagers, green behind the ears about the ministry to which we were called, we learned the ropes about it together—and are still learning!

Laneir has been an encourager, wise advisor (few equal his wisdom), confidant, and helper and has stood steadfast as a friend in all seasons.

Thank you, Leroy, for nearly a lifetime of friendship and ministry together. The journey has been swift, too swift, but filled with unspeakable fellowship, joy and blessing.

Charles Spurgeon's Challenge to Pastors to Persevere

"If there be a hundred reasons for giving up your work of faith, there are fifty thousand for going on with it. Though there are many arguments for fainting, there are far more arguments for persevering. Though we might be weary, and do sometimes feel so, let us wait upon the Lord and renew our strength, and we shall mount up with wings as eagles, forget our weariness, and be strong in the Lord and in the power of his might."[3]

"As long as there is breath in our bodies, let us serve Christ; as long as we can think, as long as we can speak, as long as we can work, let us serve Him. Let us even serve Him with our last gasp; and, if it be possible, let us try to set some work going that will glorify Him when we are dead and gone. Let us scatter some seed that may spring up when we are sleeping beneath the hillock in the cemetery."[4]

"My inference from this saying of Christ, 'It is finished,' is this: has He finished His work for me? Then I must get to work for Him, and I must persevere until I finish my work, too—not to save myself, for that is all done, but because I am saved. Now I must work for Him with all my might; and if there come discouragements, if there come sufferings, if there comes a sense of weakness and exhaustion, yet let me not give way to it; but inasmuch as He pressed on till He could say, 'It is finished,' let me press on till I too shall be able to say, 'I have finished the work which Thou gavest me to do.'"[5]

"I give you the motto: 'Go forward.' Go forward in personal attainments, forward in gifts and in grace, forward in fitness for the work, and forward in conformity to the image of Jesus."[6]

"By perseverance, the snail reached the ark."[7]

Contents

Foreword

The prophet Daniel said, "The people that do know their God shall be strong, and do exploits." Anyone who fights a good fight for God will face the opposition of Satan and the world system of which he is the prince. There will be struggles calling for stamina on the part of the faithful servant of God.

Still, in every age God has raised up strong soldiers who have done "exploits." Two such men raised up by God were the Apostle Paul and Charles Haddon Spurgeon. Although they lived in widely separated eras and served in vastly different cultures, each performed mighty deeds for the God they knew and trusted supremely.

Evangelist Frank Shivers has drawn upon the wisdom of the inspired Apostle and the inspiring pastor to glean counsel for any minister who goes to battle for God and comes face to face with the inevitable opposition. Using the experiences and the expositions of these two giants, he has gleaned instruction that will enable the struggling preacher to maintain his stamina.

This two-volume set begins with a brief but illuminating biography of Charles Spurgeon. The author consulted many previous accounts of Spurgeon's life, some of which were penned shortly after his death by people who knew him personally. Although I was involved several years ago in producing a new edition of a large biography of this "prince of preachers," I came across much new information from these lesser-known works.

Also used were the words of Spurgeon himself from the multitude of sermons he preached that were published in full during and even after his lifetime. Spurgeon was very transparent in personal references and gave clear insights into his personal struggles. His well-known success gives testimony to his stamina in the face of these struggles, and he shows in his sermons what it was that enabled him to keep going—trust in the Word of God and reliance on the strength and faithfulness of God. These are the very things that will help us today to fight a good fight.

Volume two closes with a "literary interview with Charles Spurgeon." The author poses questions as an interviewer might, and lets the preacher answer with his own words drawn from his preaching and writings. It is a closing to this work that is as fitting and worthy as it is informative.

Frank Shivers has written numerous books drawing on his decades of ministry experience, seeking to leave behind helps for those who will take up the mantle. These volumes are valuable additions to that body of work and will serve the preacher well at whatever stage of ministry he may be in.

TERRY FRALA

Murfreesboro, TN

February 2024

Preface

My introduction to Charles Haddon Spurgeon was as a college freshman (1968) when I purchased seven books of his sermons from a classmate. The books, still on my shelf, prompted the further acquisition of his writings (like *Morning and Evening; Treasury of David; Lectures to My Students; The Soul Winner;* and *An All-Round Ministry*) which have instructed, encouraged, and counseled me immensely. To say he has been to me a ministerial model and mentor throughout my ministry would be an understatement.

Not only have I been impacted by Spurgeon's sermons and books, but also by his staunch perseverance in ministerial adversity and bodily affliction—how he coped with illnesses that plagued his body continually (nearly one-third of his last twenty-two years of life was spent absent from the pulpit suffering, convalescing, or taking precautions against the return of illness[8]); the debilitating sickness of his wife, Susannah, who was a virtual shut-in; and the attacks of the liberal media, Baptist Union of Britain, and Christian antagonists of his day.

Of his trials and pain, he wrote, "I have been cast into 'waters to swim in,' which, but for God's upholding hand, would have proved waters to drown in. I have endured tribulation from many flails."[9] J. C. Carlile ends his biography of Spurgeon by saying, "The steady persistence and cheery optimism with which he faced difficulties are examples we cannot neglect. In times of depression, there is real danger of accepting the spirit of defeat. May we not turn to Spurgeon as our guide, that perchance we may secure his tenacity of purpose and serenity of spirit?"[10]

The Apostle Paul and Spurgeon are alike not only in their theology and passion for souls but also in their suffering, struggle, and stamina in Christian ministry (neither was bulletproof). Despite the hardships (though markedly different), they endured to the end, having fought a good fight each step of the way. Through the record of Paul in the Holy Scripture and the preservation of the writings of Spurgeon (sermons, memoirs, autobiography, biography, letters, diary, etc.) the minister is blessed with invaluable insights about persevering in adversity. It is my prayer that the insights gleaned from both men set forth in this two-volume set will assist ministers 'to endure suffering (hardship) as good soldiers of the Lord Jesus Christ' until their sacred task is finished.

The two volumes are interlinked. Based upon the lives of the Apostle Paul and Charles Haddon Spurgeon, Volume One identifies the struggles and pain of the preacher (that which the minister may anticipate to large measure); and Volume Two, the principles for their endurance and perseverance. The first volume is the foundation for the second and includes a biography of Spurgeon.

The prayerful intent of both is to enable the minister to say with Spurgeon, "Now I must work for Him with all my might; and if there come discouragements, if there come sufferings, if there comes a sense of weakness and exhaustion, yet let me not give way to it; but inasmuch as He pressed on till He could say, 'It is finished,' let me press on till I too shall be able to say, "I have finished the work which Thou gavest me to do."[11] Original or certifiable documentation of material used is cited (in most cases) to facilitate the reader's usage and research, and paraphrasing at large is avoided, to display Spurgeon's oratorical giftedness and anointing, and to maintain the flavor, exactness, and force of what he said.

While veteran preachers will find benefit from these books, they are aimed at ministerial students and those new to the pastorate. Respectfully, I urge all who choose to read them to bear that in mind. What may be found to be "meat" to a "raw recruit" (as Spurgeon called them) may be counted as "milk" to a master in Israel. With Spurgeon, I value the opportunity "to [humbly endeavor to] put the bread into the hands of the disciples [workers for God]," hoping "they will pass it on to the multitude."[12]

"He being dead yet speaketh" (Hebrews 11:4). Though Paul and Spurgeon's life's works are ended, they have left for preachers invaluable footprints in the sand to follow, not only to enhance their spiritual walk and work, but also to navigate the adversities that await, both enduringly and successfully (Revelation 14:13).

At the memorial service of C. H. Spurgeon for the public (February 10, 1892), Ira D. Sankey sang,

> Fading away like the stars of the morning,
> Losing their light in the glorious sun,
> Thus would we pass from the earth and its toiling,
> Only remembered by what we have done.
>
> Shall we be missed, though by others succeeded,
> Reaping the fields we in springtime have sown?
> No, for the sowers may pass from their labors,
> Only remembered by what they have done.
>
> Only the truth that in life we have spoken,
> Only the seed that on earth we have sown,
> These shall pass onward when we are forgotten,
> Fruits of the harvest and what we have done.
>
> Oh, when the Savior shall make up His jewels,
> When the bright crowns of rejoicing are won,
> Then shall His weary and faithful disciples
> All be remembered by what they have done.
> ~ Horatius Bonar (1870)

"And they overcame him by the blood of the Lamb
and by the word of their testimony, and
they did not love their lives to the death."
(Revelation 12:11 NKJV)

1

The Prince of Preachers

"In his heart, Jesus stood unapproached, unrivaled. He worshipped Him; he adored Him. He was our Lord's captive."[13]
~ Archibald Brown about C. H. Spurgeon

During Spurgeon's lifetime, Americans who returned from London were asked two questions: "Did you see the Queen?" and "Did you hear Spurgeon?"[14] Upon D. L. Moody's return from London in 1868, he was asked if he had seen various cathedrals. He replied, "No, but I've heard Spurgeon!"[15] Such was the worldwide notoriety of Spurgeon from the young age of 21.

Charles Haddon Spurgeon's conversion, and therefore his tremendous ministry, was attributable to the godly tutorage he received in the home as a child. Of that time he writes, "I was privileged with godly parents, watched with jealous eyes, scarcely ever permitted to mingle with questionable associates, warned not to listen to anything profane or licentious, and taught the way of God from my youth up. There came a time when the solemnities of eternity pressed upon me for a decision, and when a mother's tears and a father's supplications were offered to Heaven on my behalf. At such a time, had I not been helped by the grace of God, but had I been left alone to do violence to conscience and to struggle against conviction, I might perhaps have been at this moment dead, buried, and doomed, having through a course of vice brought myself to my grave; or I might have been as earnest a ringleader amongst the ungodly."[16]

Spurgeon was saved during a snowstorm at Artillery Street Primitive Methodist Chapel in Colchester, England, a town located sixty-six miles from London, on January 6, 1850, at age fifteen. (The church, formed in 1839, closed its doors following the evening service on February 24, 1957, but reopened in 1965 under the name Artillery Street Evangelical

Church. The first pastor was called three years later. Despite only a handful or so members, the church continues to operate.[17]) On April 4, 1850, he was accepted as a member of the Congregational Church at Newmarket (he refused communion until baptized).

Desirous of baptism, he sought out a Baptist minister, the nearest of which was Rev. W. W. Cantlow who resided near Isleham, to baptize him (with the blessings of his parents to "follow my own convictions"[18]). On the afternoon of May 3, 1850[19], four months after his conversion, the fifteen-year-old (almost sixteen) Spurgeon walked eight miles to the River Lark in Isleham where he was baptized by Cantlow.

In his autobiography, Spurgeon writes that at his baptism he was timid, but afterward bold. He states, "Baptism also loosed my tongue, and from that day it has never been quiet. I lost a thousand fears in the River Lark and found that 'in keeping [His commandments] there is great reward.'"[20] On the same day as his baptism, he became a Sunday school teacher, and two days later, on the afternoon of May 5, 1850, he partook of his first communion.[21] On October 2, 1850, he united with the church at Cambridge.[22] "I do not hesitate," he said, "to take the name of Baptist. But if I am asked to say what is my creed, I think I must reply, 'It is Jesus Christ.'"[23]

In the sermon "Under Arrest," Spurgeon testifies of his conversion: "Now I can never tell you how it was, but I no sooner saw Whom I was to believe than I also understood what it was to believe, and I did believe in one moment. As much as if it had never been revealed to any mortal man or written in this blessed Book, it was revealed to me by the Spirit of God that I, guilty wretch as I was, was there and then to fall at those dear feet that once were nailed to the cross and to take Jesus Christ to be my Lord and Savior, and that the moment I did so, I should be saved. I did take him as my Savior, and I am saved."[24]

In the sermon "The Truth of God's Salvation," he speaks of that glorious day: "That day when I saw Christ as my soul's salvation, the great Sacrifice for sin was, to my soul, the most real thing I had ever seen! I had real pangs of conviction and I saw a real Hell before me—and I needed a real salvation, and I grasped it as such!"[25]

He, in the sermon "Healing for the Wounded," states, "I know not the man who uttered the words that were the means of relieving my heart: 'Look unto me and be ye saved, all the ends of the earth.' I do not recollect what he said in the sermon, and I am sure I do not care to know. I found Jesus there and then, and that was enough for me."[26] It is interesting, but not surprising, that no less than three ministers claimed to have been the preacher that preached the sermon that morning, but Spurgeon did not recognize any of them as being the man to whom he listened.[27] Fewer than fifteen people were in attendance that cold winter morning to witness his conversion.[28]

I did take him as my Savior, and I am saved.
Charles Spurgeon

A companion to Spurgeon at Newmarket says of him in his early years: "He was rather small and delicate, with pale but plump face, dark brown eyes and hair, and a bright, lively manner, with a never-failing flow of conversation. He was rather deficient in muscle, did not care for cricket or other athletic games, and was timid at meeting cattle on the road."[29]

W. Y. Fullerton adds, "He was under medium height, short from loin to knee, so that he never sat far back in a chair, but with body well developed, chest deep and wide (forty-one inches over the waistcoat), head massive (twenty-three inches round) and covered with thick dark hair, which afterward turned iron grey; the ear being remarkable, its orifice opening to the front, instead of to the side, like most other ears. From his youth he was stout in build."[30] At about age thirty-five, Spurgeon's clean-shaven face became a Vandyke beard for "throat protection against London fog."[31]

His personality was "many-sided"; there were many "Spurgeon's."[32] He was an astonishing orator but a poor singer. His biographer states, "He could not sing at all."[33] W. Williams, Spurgeon's friend and former student at the Pastors' College, attested that he was "a bubbling fountain of humor."[34] He "had the most fascinating gift of laughter I ever knew in any man," Williams writes; "and he also had the greatest ability for making all who heard him laugh with him."[35] Spurgeon was never particular about attire, as long as it proved comfortable. He generally dressed in broadcloth and wore a frock coat and donned a broad-brimmed hat.[36]

Early in his ministry, he walked to preaching posts. "I walked three, five, and even eight miles out and back again in my preaching work, and I carried a dark lantern to show me the way across the fields."[37] Later he would ride in horse-drawn carriages or by train (first-class). A preacher once saw Spurgeon stepping onto the first-class carriage of a train and bragged, "I'm traveling third class, saving the Lord's money." Spurgeon replied, "I'm traveling first class, saving the Lord's servant."[38] A four-horse-drawn carriage transported him to and from the pulpit.

Photographs, drawings, and caricatures of Spurgeon show him using his entire body in preaching— hands and arms, feet in pacing the platform, and running at times from side to side (until gout and age slowed him down). Congregants say that he would occasionally take on the identity of various Bible characters in his sermons. Although he preached forty-five-minute sermons, he only took "a half-sheet of notepaper" of notes into the pulpit.[39]

And a most notable trait of Britain's and the world's great preacher was his steadfast godliness in conduct. By God's grace he never was caught up in any moral or ethical scandal that muddied his name and hindered God's work. Only months prior to his death he replied to a letter that was construed as something of a threat: "You may write my life across the sky; I have nothing to conceal."[40]

Tract distribution was Spurgeon's first Christian service. The Saturday after his baptism, as he had done for several Saturdays prior, he passed out tracts to seventy people "endeavoring to draw their attention to spiritual realities."[41] Outside of teaching Sunday school (quite successfully), Spurgeon's first "speech" was at a missionary meeting on September 10, 1849.[42] In 1853, he published his *Waterbeach Tracts*.

Spurgeon preached his first sermon at age 16 in 1850 through a little finagling by a lay preacher named James Vinter. Vinter invited Spurgeon to attend a service in a cottage at Teversham under the guise that the young man that was to preach needed the company.

Saith Spurgeon, "That was a cunningly devised sentence, if I remember it rightly, and I think I do; for at the time, in the light of that Sunday evening's revelation, I turned it over and vastly admired its ingenuity. A request to go and preach would have met with a decided negative; but merely to act as company to a good brother who did not like to be lonely, and perhaps might ask me to give out a hymn or to pray, was not at all a difficult matter, and the request, understood in that fashion, was cheerfully complied with."[43]

He continues, "We [the young preacher he thought would be preaching and himself] talked of good things, and at last I expressed my hope that he would feel the presence of God while preaching. He assured me that he had never preached in his life and could not attempt such a thing; he was looking to his young friend, Mr. Spurgeon, for that. This was a new view of the situation, and I could only reply that I was no minister, and that, even if I had been, I was quite unprepared."

The young man emphatically told Spurgeon that he himself was not a preacher and if he (Spurgeon) didn't preach, no one would. "Praying for Divine help," Spurgeon says, "I resolved to make the attempt. My text should be, 'Unto you therefore which believe He is precious,' and I would trust the Lord to open my mouth in honor of His dear Son. It seemed a great risk and a serious trial; but depending upon the power of the Holy Ghost, I would at least tell out the story of the cross and not allow the people to go home without a word."[44] Christendom will be eternally grateful for Bishop Vinter's (deceptive) maneuvering of a young Spurgeon to try out his wings to prove that he could fly. And "fly" he did.

Spurgeon at age seventeen became pastor at Waterbeach Baptist Chapel, Cambridge, in October 1851. Of the people's kindness to him he wrote to his mother in November 1852: "My congregation is as great and loving as ever. During all the time that I have been at Waterbeach, I have had a different house for my home every Sabbath day. Fifty-two families have thus taken me in, and I have still six other invitations not yet accepted."[45]

On the morning of December 18, 1853, he began a four-month trial period as pastor at New Park Street Chapel. Lewis Drummond describes that first day. "When Charles walked up the pulpit steps of New Park Street Church that December Sunday morning in 1853 with a view to becoming the church's ninth pastor, the congregation did not quite know what to think. There stood a mere boy, with a round baby face that made him look even younger than his 19 years. In build, he had to stand as tall as possible to measure five foot six inches. Somewhat thickset, like the Dutch, he had a large head, 23 inches round. His teeth protruded and were slightly crossed. His eyes did not match either. No one would ever call him handsome."[46]

On April 19, 1854, after the trial period, Spurgeon was called as pastor of the church. In response to the call Spurgeon wrote on April 28, 1854, "I have received your unanimous invitation, 'as contained in a resolution passed by you on the 19th instant' desiring me to accept the pastorate among you. No lengthened reply is required; there is but one answer to so loving and cordial an invitation. I ACCEPT IT. I have not been perplexed as to what my reply should be, for many things constrain me thus to answer."[47] At age twenty-two, he was the most renowned preacher in the world. At the start of his ministry, Spurgeon allowed himself to be called "Reverend"; in middle life, he wished no title; and in later life, he agreed to be called Pastor C. H. Spurgeon (a title in vogue among Pastors' College men).[48]

In 1861 the church relocated and was named the Metropolitan Tabernacle, a worship center that would seat 6,500 (the largest protestant church in the world at the time) to accommodate the crowds which flocked to hear him preach.[49] The church had its first service in its new location at Elephant & Castle on March 18, 1861. Spurgeon designed the pulpit platform in the new worship center to be rather large. He said, "I cannot stand like a statue when I preach. I prefer wide range both in thought and action."[50] It was from this platform that Spurgeon's first words in the Tabernacle (inaugural sermon) were uttered depicting the aim of the church: "I would propose that the subject of the ministry of this house, as long as this platform shall stand, and as long as this house shall be frequented by worshippers, shall be the person of Jesus Christ."[51] One hundred thirty years after his death, the church still abides by that standard.

Under Spurgeon's 38 years of pastoral leadership, the church expanded from 232 members to 5,311 members.[52] From April 29, 1854, to Spurgeon's death, January 31, 1892, a total of 14,460 were added to his church,[53] and at that time the membership was 5,037.[54] "For over thirty years he pastored the same church without decrease in power or appeal."[55] It is reported that Spurgeon knew the names of each of his 6,000 church members. His preaching was continuously fruitful. In a sermon preached to his church on March 1, 1868, Spurgeon said, "I do not know of any sermon preached here without conversions."[56] On a different occasion he said, "I do not come into this pulpit myself with any fear that I shall preach in vain. It does not occur to me that such a thing can happen."[57] That confidence and expectancy were the secrets of his great success.

During Spurgeon's lifetime, he preached to an estimated ten million people, not only in churches but in the open air.[58] Upon one occasion, without the benefit of a microphone and amplification, he spoke to an audience of 23,654.[59] While repairs were being made to the Tabernacle (March 24–April 21, 1867) Spurgeon spoke at the Agricultural Hall, Islington, that seated 10,000 people [20,000 attended each service[60]]. Testing the acoustics in the vast auditorium, Spurgeon shouted from the podium, "Behold the Lamb of God which taketh away the sin of the world." The words pierced the heart of a worker high in the rafters, resulting in his conversion.[61]

In the 1867 edition of *The Sword and Trowel,* a person in attendance at one of the services remarked, "Throughout, the attention was kept up, and we believe that nearly every word was distinctly heard in all parts of the building. Mr. Spurgeon's delivery was of course slow, measured, and emphatic; but nothing seemed labored, nor did the voice lose any of its accustomed music. It was clear as a bell, and from where we sat, which was three parts of the way down the building, it sounded with peculiar mellowness and sweetness."[62]

On April 20, 1898, Metropolitan Tabernacle burned while a conference was convened. Writing in the aftermath of the fire, Thomas Spurgeon said, "The massive walls of the building are still standing, but within all is ruin and devastation. Tons of blackened timber lie about or hang from the walls or other supports; debris of every conceivable thing for all sorts of uses in the work of the church strew the blackened floor, while from what remains of the massive portico one looks upon a sight never to be forgotten."[63] The church was rebuilt to the same design.

He is considered the "Prince of Preachers." Of him, B. H. Carroll, first president of Southwestern Baptist Theological Seminary (1908–1914) said, "With whom among men can you compare him? He combined the preaching power of Jonathan Edwards and Whitefield with the organizing power of Wesley and the energy, fire, and courage of Luther. In many respects he was most like Luther. In many, most like Paul."[64] Carl F. H. Henry acclaimed Charles Spurgeon "one of evangelical Christianity's immortals."[65]

George W. Truett, in an address to the Southern Baptist Convention on May 19, 1934, paid tribute to Spurgeon, stating, "These assembled thousands are of one mind that this occasion is one of the most significant and challenging of our generation. It calls to remembrance the tribute paid by Joseph Cook when Wendell Phillips went away: 'Whom God crowns, let no man discrown.' We cannot crown him; the memory of his great career crowns our civilization." He continues, "Although he came to London in an era of eminent statesmen, scholars, and preachers, he soon became far-famed above them all. There were Gladstone, John Bright, Disraeli, Browning, Tennyson, Huxley, Darwin, Dickens, Thackery, Watts, Holman Hunt, Alexander Maclaren, Joseph Parker, Canon Liddon, and John Clifford. In America were Henry Ward Beecher, Phillips Brooks, John A. Broadus, and B. H. Carroll. It is no disparagement of any of these to say that Mr. Spurgeon held and holds the primacy as a preacher."[66]

Phant and Pinson stated, "Spurgeon's oral style may have been the finest ever produced by the Christian pulpit."[67] But perhaps the greater commendation comes from a young man who wrote to his mother, after hearing Spurgeon preach, to say, "They say there were six thousand present in the tabernacle, but to me, it was as though I were alone and he was speaking to me."[68]

W. Y. Fullerton, in his biography of Spurgeon, wrote, "He preached from every book of the Bible, from some texts several times. It is remarkable that the sermons unpublished at the time of his death, like the published sermons, even when they deal with the same theme, avoid repetition. Of course, on occasion, when preaching away from home, he would repeat a sermon, generally the sermon of the previous Sabbath, but even in such cases, such was the productiveness of his mind that he would sometimes prefer to preach an original sermon."[69]

Spurgeon staunchly embraced the infallibility of Scripture. He testified, "The thoughts of God are in no degree perverted by being uttered in the words of men. The testimony of God, on the human as well as the divine side, is perfect and infallible; and however others may think of it, we shall not cease to believe in it with all our heart and soul. The Holy Spirit has made no mistake, either in history, physics, theology, or anything else. God is a greater Scientist than any of those who assume that title. If the human side had tainted the lesser statements, we could not be sure of the greater.…But the human side has communicated no taint whatever to Holy Scripture."[70]

And he preached *all* the Word. In the sermon "Preach the Gospel," he declared, "Am I to put His words in the scale and say, 'This is good, and that is evil?' Am I to take God's Bible and sever it and say, 'This is husk, and this is wheat?' Am I to cast away any one truth and say, 'I dare not preach it?' No! God forbid. Whatsoever is written in God's Word is written for our instruction, and the whole of it is profitable, either for reproof, or for consolation, or for edification in righteousness.

No truth of God's Word ought to be withheld, but every portion of it preached in its own proper order."[71]

Albert Mohler wrote of his preaching, "But whatever the text—Old Testament or New Testament—Spurgeon would find his way to the Gospel of the Savior on the cross. And that Gospel was put forth with the full force of substitutionary atonement and with warnings of eternal punishment."[72]

Spurgeon professed to be a premillennialist. In the sermon "Justification and Glory," he plainly said, "I conceive that the advent will be premillennial; that is, He will come first, and then will come the millennium as the result of His personal reign upon earth."[73] Further substantiation of his embracing this eschatological view is historically documented by his signing an Evangelical Baptist "statement of doctrine" which included "affirmation of the premillennial Advent."[74]

The first convert of the London preacher was Hannah Spalding (age 49), saved during his 100th sermon (1851), "Sinners Must Be Punished" (Psalm 9:17). Of getting the news of the conversion from a deacon three weeks later Spurgeon said: "How my heart leapt for joy when I heard tidings of my first convert. Oh, if anybody had said to me, 'Someone has left you 20,000 pounds,' I should not have given a snap of my fingers for it compared with the joy which I felt when I was told that God had saved a soul through my ministry. I felt like a boy who had earned his first guinea [coin composed of a one-quarter ounce of gold] or like the diver who had brought up a rare pearl. I prize each one whom God has given me, but I prize this woman the most. She is the first seal to my ministry and a precious one."[75] What perseverance he displayed to preach over one hundred times without a single convert!

The "very first money" Spurgeon made for pulpit services in London was invested in a set of commentaries by Thomas Scott, of which latter he said, "To me he has seldom given a thought, and I have almost discontinued consulting him."[76]

"His work," Spurgeon said, "has always been popular, is very judicious, thoroughly sound and gracious; but for suggestiveness and pith is not comparable to Matthew Henry."[77]

Spurgeon possessed a photographic memory and virtually total recall which enabled him to preach with few notes.[78] The exceptional memory gave him what he called "a shelf in my mind" to store everything consumed for future use. It is said that he knew the contents of all the 12,000 volumes (1,000 printed before the year 1700) in his library.[79] He was able to pull from his hours of reading and study at will when needed while preaching.

Spurgeon's first printed sermon was one preached at New Park Street Chapel on August 20, 1854 ("Is It Not Wheat Harvest Today?"). The first sermon to be printed on a weekly basis was entitled "The Immutability of God" and delivered at New Park Street Chapel on January 7, 1855 (the weekly sermon continued for sixty-two years with the last published on May 10, 1917). "There has been nothing in all sermon literature to equal this record [longevity], either in numbers or circulation."[80]

The sermons were transcribed as he preached them by stenographers present in the congregation on Sundays (although he wrote the sermons out fully in manuscript form, what he took into the pulpit was a notecard with a brief outline sketch[81]) and on Mondays revised by Spurgeon. The changes he made are notable. (A simile of a page of a sermon Spurgeon revised is depicted in *C. H. Spurgeon's Autobiography,* Vol. 2: "The Full Harvest," 324). "A Stanza of Deliverance" was revised on January 9, 1892, and proved to be the last to be edited before Spurgeon's death. How fitting that it was done with the greatest of ease and joy. "Never did he revise a sermon with greater ease or more delight. His pen seemed to fly along the pages."[82]

Charles Ray, a biographer of Spurgeon, states with regard to the publication of his weekly sermons, "If all that have been issued [published] were to be placed side by side, they would stretch a distance of 13,889 miles, or more than half way round the globe."[83] By the time of his death, Spurgeon had preached 3,962 sermons.[84] See the endnote cited for an alphabetical index to all of Spurgeon's sermons with text, except the early years.[85]

F. B. Meyer like many other ministers was impacted by Spurgeon's printed sermons: "I can never tell my indebtedness to them. As I read them week by week in my young manhood, they gave me a grip of the Gospel that I can never lose and gave me an ideal of its presentation in nervous, transparent, and forcible language which has colored my entire ministry."[86] Spurgeon testified that "seldom a day passed, and certainly never a week" without letters arriving informing him of salvation decisions as a result of reading his weekly sermon.[87]

Outside the publication of his sermons, Spurgeon authored about 150 books,[88] including *The Treasury of David,* a seven-volume commentary on the Psalms (Spurgeon's favorite biblical book). Its last volume was completed in 1885, twenty years after the project began. One hundred thirty years after his death there are more titles by him in print than by any other Christian author, living or dead.

In the sermon "Watching to See," Spurgeon explains why he wrote so much (and why preachers should, if so gifted). He says, "When you and I have seen or heard anything which God has revealed to us, let us go and write it or make it known by some other means. God has not put the treasure into the earthen vessel merely for the vessel's own sake, but that the treasure may afterwards be poured out from it, that others thereby may be enriched."[89]

Spurgeon was devoted to long days (18 hours) and short nights in Christian service. A typical week's work for

Spurgeon is cited in the appendix. Saith he, "If we are not laborers, we are not true stewards; for we are to be examples of diligence to the King's household. I like Adam Clarke's precept: 'Kill yourself with work, and then pray yourselves alive again.' We shall never do our duty either to God or man if we are sluggards. Yet some, who are always busy, may still be unfaithful, if all that they do is done in a jaunty [jolly], trifling manner."[90]

Despite the daily intense schedule, he read six books a week (Christian classics, history, biography, and fiction).[91] William Wright, a close friend of Spurgeon's, asserts that he would master five or six large books at one sitting.[92] It's noteworthy that he read *Pilgrim's Progress* over 100 times.[93] Dr. Richard Glover of Bristol, in W. Y. Fullerton's biography of Spurgeon, asserts, "To listen to his talk on books one would think that he had done nothing but read in the library all his life, and to mark his publications would fancy that he had done nothing but write."[94] Unknown to many is that, in addition to Spurgeon's oratory and writing giftedness, he was astonishing talented in writing poetry.

Spurgeon served the mega Metropolitan Tabernacle church without an associate until 1868, when James Spurgeon, his brother, became copastor. In 1891 William Stott was appointed as assistant minister for the year. In a letter to Stott about the appointment, Spurgeon said, "It would be a great relief to me if I knew that someone was on the spot to take the pulpit should I suddenly fall."[95] On Sunday night, April 26, 1891, that sadly happened, and Stott picked up where Spurgeon had left off and finished the service. This bespeaks the value of having a preaching associate, especially if one is ill, as Spurgeon was.

Spurgeon's liberality was laudable. He believed strongly that "to get, we must give."[96] In the sermon "Black Clouds and Bright Blessings," Spurgeon asserts, "God has a way of giving by the cartloads to those who give away by shovelfuls."[97] A longstanding tradition at Metropolitan Tabernacle was that the pastor never made an appeal for money to a cause without himself making a donation.[98] Often it was Spurgeon who gave the largest gift.

From the sale of books and sermons, he earned in today's U.S. dollars $26,144,925.33.[99] The amount he earned from speaking engagements is unknown. He gave so liberally to the 66 institutions he founded (orphanages, a college, almshouses, nursing homes, Sunday schools for the blind and children, book fund, policemen ministries, etc.), to other causes (for example, when Waterbeach Chapel burned in 1861 he paid for its rebuilding personally), and to the church that at his death, though debt free, his financial worth was only £2,000 (the equivalent of $235,560 today) per the *Nottingham Evening Post,* March 31, 1892.[100] In September 1890, sixteen months before his death, he exclaimed, "Gold is nothing but dust to a dying man."[101]

A little-known fact is that he refused to be paid as pastor at Metropolitan Tabernacle (after about the first three months) and personally financed much (nearly two million dollars) of the construction of the Pastors' College he founded at New Park Street Chapel in 1855 with one student—Thomas Medhurst, a convert of Spurgeon's ministry.[102] Additionally, he often covered the college's weekly operation cost out of his own pocket ($11,778),[103] paid tuition costs for the students, and frequently bought them suits to preach in.[104]

Antagonists of Spurgeon said the college was nothing short of a mill to manufacture preachers, despite Spurgeon's making clear that such was not his purpose, nor that of the college.[105] It was to train those who were called. The school sprang into existence upon Spurgeon witnessing the success of the training of Medhurst. Speaking to the church on May 19, 1861, he said, "So useful was that brother, that I was induced to take another, and another, and another."[106]

In the preface to the book *Commenting and Commentaries,* he wrote of the Pastors' College, "The Institution is intended to aid useful preachers in obtaining a better education. It takes no man to make him a minister, but requires that its pupils should, as a rule, have exercised their gifts for at least two years, and have won souls to Jesus. These we receive, however poor or backward they may be, and our endeavors are all turned toward the one aim: that they should be instructed in the things of God, furnished for their work, and practiced in the gift of utterance."[107]

The Pastors' College, of which Spurgeon was both founder and President (though he himself received no formal theological education) witnessed 900 graduates before his death.[108] That number of alumni is significant, for it meant that by 1892 one out of five Baptist ministers in England were alumni of the College.[109] Prior to Spurgeon's death, alumni of the College planted over 200 churches (80 in the London area), administered 100,000 baptisms, and received 80,000 new members into their congregations.[110]

The day-to-day administration of the College fell to James Spurgeon and its Principal. Spurgeon trusted George Rogers in the early years for the bulk of the teaching at the institution. Spurgeon himself delivered "Lectures to My Students" on Friday afternoons. The college moved to the premises of the Metropolitan Tabernacle in 1861 (from 1861—1873 the college met in rooms under the Metropolitan Tabernacle) and into its new residence in September 1874.

Thomas Johnson, a black man born into slavery (a slave for 28 years) in the United States heard of Spurgeon's fierce opposition to slavery. By divine providence Johnson became not only the first black man to attend Spurgeon's Pastors' College (reported to class December 3, 1876[111]) to prepare for work as a missionary in Africa, but Spurgeon's friend as well. In fact, such a friend, purportedly, that he was with Spurgeon when he drew his last breath.[112]

Spurgeon College, as it is now named, continues the work Spurgeon founded, but with diminished links to the Metropolitan Tabernacle.[113] For insight into the curriculum and schedule and other interesting data of the Pastors' College under Spurgeon's presidency, access the link cited in this endnote.[114] It was most fitting that the great warrior's casket was first placed in the Pastors' College upon its arrival on February 8, 1892, from Mentone, France (close to 10 PM that night students took the casket to the Metropolitan Tabernacle).

In 1866 at a Monday evening prayer meeting at the Metropolitan Tabernacle, Spurgeon told his people, "Dear friends, we are a huge church and should be doing more for the Lord in this great city. I want us tonight to ask Him to send us some new work. And if we need money to carry it on, let us pray that the means also be sent."[115]

Unknown to Spurgeon, God immediately began to work in answer to that prayer. A widow, Anne Hillyard, had read Spurgeon's article in *The Sword and Trowel* entitled "The Holy War of the Present Hour" which cited the need for greater ministry to children, and it prompted her to invest in a work dear to her heart, fatherless boys. Not knowing how to proceed, she asked a friend for the name of a reliable person to undertake such an enterprise, and the name of Spurgeon was immediately given.[116]

A few days afterward Spurgeon received a letter from the widow stating she wanted to contribute the sum of 20,000 pounds ($100,000 at that time) for an orphanage to train and educate orphan boys, and asking for his assistance. At her behest, William Higgs and Spurgeon paid a visit to her home to discuss the matter. Spurgeon suggested she give the money to George Müller's orphanage, but she was insistent that he use the money in London to establish the work. As Spurgeon and Higgs left her home, they remarked one to the other how God was evidently answering the prayer uttered a few nights earlier.

Within a month two and a half acres of land were purchased close to the church, and in time the facility was erected that housed 250 boys and 250 girls.[117] September 9, 1869, the doors to the orphanage opened (first to boys) and remained so until the war in 1939 forced the children's evacuation. The home continued temporarily in other locations until the Spurgeon home opened in Birchington, Kent in 1951. The orphanage closed in 1979 when the children were sent to smaller foster homes.[118] The work Spurgeon started in 1867 continues through the international charity Spurgeons, operating over 50 children's centers across the UK.[119]

January 8, 1856, Spurgeon and Susannah were married at the New Park Street Chapel, London. He called her Susie, along with "wifey," and she in turn called him *Tirshatha*, a title used by the Judean governor under the Persian empire, meaning "Your Excellency."[120] At age 33 medical issues plagued Susannah, leaving her an invalid for the rest of her life. She wrote, "It was the ever settled purpose of my married life that I should never hinder him in his work for the Lord, never try to keep him from fulfilling his engagements, never plead my own ill health as a reason why he should remain at home with me....I thank God, now, that He enabled me to carry out this determination."[121]

Thomas, her son, wrote of her labor for Charles: "She consoled him in his sorrows and disappointments; she succored him 'as an angel of God' when men spoke all manner of evil against him falsely; she nursed him in his sicknesses; she entertained his guests. She even reproduced for him a sermon he had delivered in his sleep from a text he failed to expound satisfactorily before he retired to rest." Note: the sermon he preached in his sleep that she recounted to him he preached that very Sunday, April 13, 1856 ("A Willing People and an Immutable Leader").[122]

Susannah was affectionally known as "Mother" to the students at the Pastors' College.[123] Charles and she extended gracious hospitality to the college students in their home.[124] Ray Rhodes writes, "Charles could not have met the demands of ministry, have written so prolifically, and have left such an incredible mark in history without the encouragement of Susie."[125]

Upon Charles's death, she remained a member of the Metropolitan Tabernacle until her death on October 22, 1903. At her graveside, Archibald Brown stated: "Farewell, sister! We praise God for thee. We are grateful for the help thou didst bring thy husband in his ceaseless toil and hard-fought battle."[126] Her tombstone, next to Charles', bears the inscription:

Since all that I meet shall work for my good,
The bitter is sweet; the medicine is food.
Though painful at present, wilt cease before long.
And then, oh! how pleasant, the conqueror's song.

Another key factor to Spurgeon's success at the Metropolitan Tabernacle was the support of the nine deacons. Speaking on behalf of the church's other deacons, William Olney said to him, "Dear pastor, but it is because we have such absolute confidence in your leadership that we are ready to follow you anywhere. You have never misled us yet, and we do not believe you ever will do so."[127] His deacons loved him to the degree that one, presumably speaking for all, said that if he encountered a ditch, they will fill it with their bodies so he could cross over. In hearing that, Spurgeon responded, "That was grand talk."[128] And said of them, "At every remembrance of these brethren we thank God. Some ministers have found their trials in their deacons; it is but right to say that we find in them our greatest comfort, and we earnestly desire that every church should share in an equal blessing."[129]

"The greatest man of Apostolic times," stated Spurgeon, "was the apostle Paul. He was always great in everything. If you consider him as a sinner, he was exceeding sinful; if you regard him as a persecutor, he was exceeding mad against the Christians, and persecuted them even unto strange cities; if you take him as a convert, his conversion was the most notable one of which we read, worked by miraculous power and by the direct voice of Jesus speaking from Heaven—'Saul, Saul, why persecutest thou me?' If we take him simply as a Christian, he was an extraordinary one, loving his Master more than others and seeking more than others to exemplify the grace of God in his life. But if you take him as an apostle and as a preacher of the Word, he stands out pre-eminent as the prince of preachers and a preacher to kings—for he preached before Agrippa, he preached before Nero Caesar—he stood before emperors and kings for Christ's name's sake. It was the characteristic of Paul that whatever he did, he did with all his heart."[130]

From his diary, given to Susannah after their marriage but not opened until his death, he wrote on May 9, 1850, of the passion to be like the Apostle Paul: "Make me to be an eminent servant of Thine, and to be blessed with power to serve Thee like Thy great servant Paul." And on June 7: "Could I be like Paul, how honored I should be!"[131] God gave him the desire of his heart, as history attests. B. H. Carroll, in a eulogy for the great preacher a week after his death, asked, "How do you account for Spurgeon? The answer is...God."[132]

Spurgeon preached his final sermon at the Tabernacle ("The Statute of David for the Sharing of the Spoil") on June 7, 1891. On October 26, 1891, accompanied by five others (Susie, Harrald, Allison, and J. A. and Mrs. Spurgeon) Spurgeon traveled to Mentone, France. Only weeks prior to his death in the sitting room at the Hotel Beau Rivage in Mentone (the hotel remains in business), the great London preacher said to friends (January 1, 1892): "We would have it so happen when our life's history is written. Whoever reads it will not think of us as self-made men but as the handiwork of God in whom His grace is magnified. Not in us may men see the clay but the potter's hands. They said of one, 'He is a fine preacher,' but of another they said, 'We never notice how he preaches but we feel that God is great.'"

He concluded with saying, "We wish our whole life to be a sacrifice, an altar of incense continually smoking with sweet perfume unto the Most High.…The vista of a praiseful life will never close, but continue throughout eternity. From psalm to psalm, from hallelujah to hallelujah, we will ascend the hill of the Lord, until we come to the holiest of all, where, with veiled faces, we will bow before the Divine Majesty in the bliss of endless adoration."[133] Amen and amen.

On January 17, 1892, in the same sitting room, Spurgeon shared his final remarks, reading excerpts from his sermon on Psalm 73:28 and Exposition from Matthew 15:21–28. The last hymn that he sang on earth was "The Sands of Time Are Sinking."[134]

Spurgeon's last act and last message was a telegram he sent to the Tabernacle (January 26): "*Self and wife, 100 pounds, hearty thanksgiving towards Tabernacle General Expenses. Love to all friends.*"[135] Shortly later he succumbed to kidney failure and became unconscious, remaining so until he was ushered into the presence of God on January 31 at 11:05 PM. Susannah, his wife for thirty-six years, had been gazing into the sky at the planets Jupiter and Venus, which were unusually bright that night. Speaking of Charles, she said to Joseph W. Harrald (Spurgeon's private secretary), "I wonder what he thinks of those planets now."

Harrald replied, "If they are inhabited, he has asked the Lord to let him go, that he may preach the Gospel there."

"No doubt of it," was her reply. And she added, "For how often he said that, when he got to Heaven, he would stand at the corner of one of its streets and proclaim to the angels the old, old story of Jesus and His love!"[136] In the room with Susannah and Harrald when the great preacher breathed his last breath were Mrs. Thorne, Mr. Allison, Mr. Samuel, and

Dr. Fitzhenry. They together knelt and thanked God for Spurgeon's great life.[137]

The tribute and funeral services were at the Tabernacle February 9–11, with the interment on Thursday, February 11 at West Norwood Cemetery. Viewing by the public flowed smoothly in two lines from 7 AM–7 PM on Tuesday, February 9, with memorial services Wednesday, February 10, morning for church members, afternoon for ministers and students, evening for Christian workers, and night (10:00 PM) for the general public. Thursday morning, at 11 AM the funeral service was conducted.[138]

Atop the olivewood casket was Spurgeon's Bible (the one used so long at the Tabernacle) opened at Isaiah 45:22: "Look unto me, and be ye saved, all the ends of the earth," the text which was used to bring about his conversion on January 6, 1850.[139] It is said that no less than 100,000 people attended the interment.[140] The procession stretched for two miles.

Archibald Brown, the primary speaker at Spurgeon's funeral, said in part: "Hard Worker in the field, thy toil is ended! Straight has been the furrow thou hast ploughed. No looking back has marred thy course. Harvests have followed thy patient sowing, and Heaven is already rich with thine ingathered sheaves, and shall still be enriched through the years yet lying in eternity....Loving president, prince of preachers, brother beloved, faithful servant, dear Spurgeon, we bid thee not 'Farewell,' but only for a little while 'Goodnight.'...We praise God *for* thee; and by the blood of the everlasting covenant, we hope and expect to praise God *with* thee. Amen."[141]

Fittingly, eight students were specifically chosen from the Pastors' College which Spurgeon founded to carry the prized coffin with his Bible atop to its gravesite.[142] Heber Evans in his funeral eulogy of Spurgeon sums up the legacy of the great preacher. "But there is one Charles Haddon Spurgeon whom we cannot bury; there is not earth enough in Norwood to bury him—the Spurgeon of history."[143]

Eighteen years earlier in the sermon "The Time Is Short," Spurgeon envisioned the scene of that February 11 day: "In a little while, there will be a great concourse of people in the streets. Methinks I hear someone enquiring, 'What are all these people waiting for?' 'Do you not know? He is to be buried today.' 'And who is that?' 'It is Spurgeon.' 'What! the man that preached at the Tabernacle?' 'Yes; he is to be buried today.' That will happen very soon; and when you see my coffin carried to the silent grave, I should like every one of you, whether converted or not, to be constrained to say, 'He did earnestly urge us, in plain and simple language, not to put off the consideration of eternal things. He did entreat us to look to Christ. Now he is gone; our blood is not at his door if we perish."[144]

D. L. Moody speaking at Metropolitan Tabernacle's Jubilee service on June 18, 1884 (the celebration of Spurgeon's 50th birthday), after giving wondrous praise for Spurgeon's life and the ministry, said something applicable to every preacher today, "But let me just say this, if God can use Mr. Spurgeon, why should He not use the rest of us, and why should we not all just lay ourselves at the Master's feet and say to Him, 'Send me; use me'? It is not Mr. Spurgeon who does the work, after all; it is God. He is as weak as any other man apart from his Lord."

Then just moments prior to concluding he said, "Mr. Spurgeon, God bless you! I know that you love me, but I assure you that I love you a thousand times more than you can ever love me, because you have been such a blessing to me, while I have been a very little blessing to you. I have read your sermons for twenty-five years. You are never going to die. *Bear in mind, friends, that our dear brother is to live forever.* We may never meet together again in the flesh [they didn't]; but, by the blessing of God, I will meet you up yonder."[145]

Moody's prophesy has been proven true on both accounts. Spurgeon lives on through his books and sermons. And soon we, as Moody, will meet up in Glory with him whom many call "The Prince of Preachers," "of whom the world was not worthy" (Hebrews 11:38).

Found in Spurgeon's desk after his death written in his own handwriting were these words:[146]

No cross, no crown; no loss, no gain;
They, too, must suffer who would reign.
He best can part with life without a sigh,
Whose daily living is to daily die.
Youth pleads for age; age pleads for rest;
Who pleads for Heaven will plead the best.
Poor they may live, but rich they die,
Whose treasure is laid up on high.
Oh, the sweet joy that sentence gives,
"I know that my Redeemer lives!"
We cannot, Lord, Thy purpose see,
But all is well that's done by Thee. ~ C. H. Spurgeon

On a Friday, Spurgeon at the Pastors' College said, "When I am gone all sorts people will write my life. They will have some difficulty in accounting for the position God has given me. I can tell you two reasons why I am what I am. My mother and the truth of my message."[147]

"My life seems to me like a fairy dream. I am often both amazed and dazed with its mercies and its love. How good God has been to me! I used to think that I should sing among the saints above as loudly as any, for I owe so much to the grace of God."[148] ~ C. H. Spurgeon

2
The Preacher's Call

"Brethren, I beseech you, crave Moses' place, but tremble as you take it."[149] ~ C. H. Spurgeon

Paul testified to Agrippa of the surety of his call (Acts 26:16–18) declaring that he was "not disobedient" to [that] heavenly calling (Acts 26:19). And Spurgeon said, "It would have been a fearful thing for me to have occupied the watchman's place without having received the watchman's commission."[150] Let him that contemplates entrance into the ministry make proof of the calling, for without it *fainting* will result when trials and suffering arise. "It will be a lamentable thing for us," saith Spurgeon, "to start in our course without due examination, for if so, we may have to leave it in disgrace."[151] There are ten signposts that unitedly indicate a call to ministry.

Inner compulsion. He that is called possesses a raging thirst to preach. It's a divine constraint birthed in him by the Holy Spirit that is unshakeable. He feels he has no alternative but to preach. This is why Spurgeon said, "If you can do anything else do it. If you can stay out of the ministry, stay out of the ministry." "If any…could be content to be a newspaper editor, or a grocer, or a farmer, or a doctor, or a lawyer, or a senator, or a king, in the name of Heaven and earth let him go his way; he is not the man in whom dwells the Spirit of God in its fulness, for a man so filled with God would utterly weary of any pursuit but that for which his inmost soul pants."[152]

In agreement, Martyn Lloyd-Jones said, "I would say that the only man who is called to preach is the man who cannot do anything else, in the sense that he is not satisfied with anything else. This call to preach is so put upon him, and such pressure comes to bear upon him, that he says, 'I can do nothing else; I must preach.'"[153] J. H. Jowett states, "I would affirm my own conviction that in all genuine callings to the ministry there is a sense of the divine initiative, a solemn communication of the divine will, a mysterious feeling of commission, which leaves a man no alternative, but which sets him in the road of this vocation bearing the ambassage of a servant and instrument of the eternal God."[154]

He who is divinely called cries with Paul, "For necessity is laid upon me; yea, woe is unto me, if I preach not the Gospel!" (1 Corinthians 9:16). In the call God puts a 'fire in the bones' to preach that neither time, trouble nor tribunal can quench. Martin Lloyd-Jones testified, "It was God's hand that laid hold of me, and drew me out, and separated me to this work."[155] And J. C. Ryle said of his call, "I became a clergyman because I felt shut up to do it and saw no other course of life open to me."[156]

In the sermon "Preach the Gospel," Spurgeon says, "A man who has really within him the inspiration of the Holy Ghost calling him to preach cannot help it. He must preach. Friends may check him, foes criticize him, despisers sneer at him; the man is indomitable. He must preach if he has the call of Heaven"[157] W. Griffith-Thomas said of the divine call, "It must be in some way the immediate appeal of God to the soul: 'Son, go work today in My vineyard.'"[158] In the sermon "Harvest Men Wanted," Spurgeon says, "May the Lord push men out, thrust them out, drive them out, and compel them to preach the Gospel. For unless they preach by a divine compulsion, there will be no spiritual compulsion in their ministry upon the hearts of others."[159]

Compliance with scriptural requirements. The call to ministry always meshes with its biblical criteria. The requisite traits ("musts") for ministry include being converted, living above reproach (unimpeachable reputation—the overarching requirement[160]), being holy ("The hand," saith Gregory, "that means to make another clean must not itself be dirty"), showing self-control, being hospitable (not snobbish but inviting, welcoming to the saved and unsaved alike), not quick-tempered (gentle, respectful in dealing with people), humble (senses unworthiness, not puffed up with pride), the husband of one wife (says Spurgeon, "We will add that our surprise is all the greater when women of piety mount the pulpit, for they are acting in plain defiance of the command of the Holy Spirit, written by the pen of the apostle Paul"[161]) and exhibiting grace to live the Christian life at home, being apt (skillful) to teach (preaching and teaching of God's Word is the pastor's primary duty[162]), not a novice (new convert), zealous for souls (saith Spurgeon, "If the Lord gives you no zeal for souls, keep to the lapstone or the trowel, but avoid the pulpit"[163]), manifesting a servant's heart, embracing sound doctrine, not being quarrelsome (an agitator promoting disunity), abstaining from alcohol, and not being greedy for money (love for God and people, not wealth, motivates his service). See 1 Timothy 3:1–7; Titus1:5–9; 1 Peter 5:2–3; 2 Timothy 4:5, Philippians 2:15, and Romans 12:16.

Church confirmation. It is the "preacher's" home church (its spiritual leaders and membership at large) that is charged with the task of commissioning him to the ministry (Romans 10:13–15). Prime and Begg state, "No church is better able to confirm a call to the ministry than a man's home church—it is the natural and appropriate proving ground. He should submit himself, therefore, to the spiritual leadership of his church fellowship, asking them to test his call."[164] Saith Spurgeon, "That none of you can be pastors without the loving consent of the flock; and therefore, this will be to you a practical indicator if not a correct one."[165] The failure of the church to see the biblical signs and marks and qualifications of a man seeking the pastorate ought to be considered an indicator to him not to pursue it further.[166]

Witness of the saints. Evidence of a call will be outwardly manifested. Candid, discerning advice from the spiritual based upon observation of the person's life and giftedness will help dissipate the fog enveloping God's call. "Yet this appeal," says

Spurgeon, "is not final nor infallible, and is only to be estimated in proportion to the intelligence and piety of those consulted. Considerable weight is to be given to the judgment of men and women who live near to God, and in most instances their verdict will not be a mistaken one."[167] The saint consulted occupies a most important place, for should he voice the wrong opinion an *unfit* man may pursue the ministry or a *fit* man walk away from it. Therefore, Paul exhorts the saint consulted not to be in a hurry in making that determination (1 Timothy 5:22).

Readiness to suffer. "You must be fitted to lead," instructs Spurgeon, "prepared to endure, and able to persevere."[168] "We must try whether we can endure browbeating, weariness, slander, jeering, and hardship; and whether we can be made the offscouring of all things, and be treated as nothing for Christ's sake. If we can endure all these, we have some of those points which indicate the possession of the rare qualities which should meet in a true servant of the Lord Jesus Christ."[169]

Ability to preach. To students at the Pastors' College Spurgeon said: "Still, a man must not consider that he is called to preach until he has proved that he can speak….If a man be called to preach, he will be endowed with a degree of speaking ability, which he will cultivate and increase. If the gift of utterance be not there in a measure at the first, it is not likely that it will ever be developed."[170] "Whatever you may know," continues Spurgeon, "you cannot be truly efficient ministers if you are not 'apt to teach.'"[171] Note, no man is expected to teach or preach like a seasoned minister at the first, but there will be evidence of giftedness. W. Griffith-Thomas states, "God never calls without equipping, and the very fact of equipment proves the call."[172] Saith Spurgeon, "We [also] need *spiritual qualifications* graces which must be wrought in us by the Lord himself. Other things are precious, but this is priceless; we must be rich towards God."[173]

Alignment of spiritual markers. Spiritual markers are places and reference points that identify a transition, decision, or direction when God clearly gave guidance.[174] In looking at these markers, one can readily see the direction God is moving his life. These markers are important in understanding God's guidance. A good help in knowing that you are walking in the will of God when you encounter another marker (for instance a call to ministry) is to look at the previous markers. If they all seem to point in the same direction as the new marker, then it is most likely that you are moving in the right direction.

Open doors to minister. Spontaneous opportunities to preach and minister serve as a *likely* indicator of the call to preach. It is the testimony of some that their call was manifest in being "thrust" into ministry service by the Holy Spirit.

Personal fruitfulness. The blessing and favor of God upon a man's religious efforts (soul winning, preaching, teaching, etc.) is a sure signpost of a possible call. Following Spurgeon's conversion, he taught Sunday school with such effectualness that he was invited to address the whole school. A burden for ministry overtook him to the point that he prayed, "Make me Thy faithful servant, O my God; may I honor Thee in my day and generation and be consecrated forever to Thy service."[175] Spurgeon's display of mighty giftedness alerted others and himself of the divine summons to ministry. Note, saith Spurgeon, "He who does not serve God where he is would not serve God anywhere else."[176]

Seal of the Holy Spirit. W. Griffith-Thomas states that the call is primarily the "internal work of the Holy Spirit."[177] The Holy Spirit calls and confirms the call to the open and waiting heart. The Spirit told the church at Antioch to set apart Barnabas and Paul for the ministry (Acts 13:2). When examined for ordination regarding my call to ministry by a group of ministers the question was asked what I would do if they declined to affirm my call. I replied, "I will preach anyway." This I could say not solely because of holy constraint to preach and biblical and experiential indicators of a call, but mostly by the inner confirmation of the Holy Spirit that I was called (Romans 8:16a).

To one degree or the other, each of these ten indicators will be present in the life of him that is called to ministry. Patiently wait upon the Lord in prayer to confirm the call. Don't rush the decision. Wait until you hear the rumbling of the "mulberry trees" (2 Samuel 5:24). It will come in its proper time if it is to come.

John Newton well says, "If it be the Lord's will to bring you into His ministry, He has already appointed your place and service, and though you know it not at present, you shall at a proper time. If you had the talents of an angel, you could do no good with them till His hour is come, and till He leads you to the people whom he has determined to bless by your means. It is very difficult to restrain ourselves within the bounds of prudence here when our zeal is warm; a sense of the love of Christ upon our hearts, and a tender compassion for poor sinners is ready to prompt us to break out too soon, but he that believeth shall not make haste."[178] Wait, I say, upon the Lord.

> To me is this grace GIVEN that I should preach.
> Ephesians 3:8

Upon confirmation of the call, "go forth armed from head to foot with armor of proof."[179] George Kulp states, "There will be a time come in the ministry of every preacher when he will be glad 'that God put him in the ministry,' that he did not seek the office, for with the knowledge that it was God who called him there will come the assurance that He who called will also equip, defend, accompany and energize His servant, rendering him effective wherever his lot may be cast. 'To me is this grace GIVEN that I should preach'" (Ephesians 3:8).[180]

The church needs more divinely "called out" ministers. Concerning God's question in Isaiah 6:8, "Whom shall I send, and who will go for us?" John Wesley wrote George Whitfield asking, "What, Mr. Whitefield, if thou art that man?"[181] Whitefield shook a continent for God. I ask that same question: "What if thou art that man?" What if God is calling you to the pastorate, mission field, or vocational evangelism? Stand ready to respond with Isaiah, Paul, and Spurgeon, saying "Here am I. Send me; send me."

3
The Preacher's Unworthiness

"I feel myself to be a lump of unworthiness, a mass of corruption, and a heap of sin, apart from His almighty love."[182] ~ C. H. Spurgeon

Both Paul's and Spurgeon's feelings of ministerial inadequacy were birthed from their lofty view of the holiness of God, as well as seeing their own inabilities, wretchedness, impotence, and terrible sacred assignment. Saith Paul, "Not that we are sufficient of ourselves to think any thing as of ourselves; but our sufficiency is of God; who also *hath made us able ministers*" (2 Corinthians 3:5–6). Paul, though a chosen vessel blessed with multiple gifts, felt that he was "nothing" (2 Corinthians 12:11), that he was "less than the least of all saints" (Ephesians 3:8). Further he exclaimed, "For I am the least worthy of the apostles, and not fit to be called an apostle, because I at one time fiercely oppressed and violently persecuted the church of God" (1 Corinthians 15:9 AMP).

Albert Barnes states, "Paul could never forget that, as a man who has been profane and a scoffer, when he becomes converted, can never forget the deep guilt of his former life. The effect will be to produce humility and a deep sense of unworthiness ever onward."[183] Paul emphatically says, "I refuse to allow the heavy baggage of the guilt and shame of past sin to weigh me down, therefore I discard it at the Cross so that I might put forth every particle of my focus and strength in running wide open the race to win the trophy of Christ's approval" (Philippians 3:13).

George W. Truett said, "If Paul had not learned how to forget those awful sins that mastered him back yonder, if he had not learned how to get past them, then he would have gone with an accusing conscience and broken spirit clear to his grave."[184] Likewise, if the preacher doesn't get past his mistakes and failures life will be full of despair, the conscience torturous and Christian work handcuffed. Don't let the past define your future. Oswald Chambers states, "Never let the sense of past failure defeat your next step."[185]

Sin says we are utterly unworthy to bear His name and receive His holy calling. But the Bible says, "The blood of Jesus Christ His son cleanseth us from all sin" (1 John 1:7) and "though your sins be as scarlet, they shall be as white as snow" (Isaiah 1:18). Of the minister Spurgeon says, "He is never satisfied with himself, for he forms a right estimate of himself, and he weeps to think that he is so poor an instrument for so good a Master."[186]

Spurgeon battled the feeling of unworthiness. He said, "Satan tells me I am unworthy; but I always was unworthy, and yet God has long loved me."[187] In the sermon "The Trumpet Blast and Church Member Warning" he testified, "When I sit down and think of myself, I am, to my own self, a wonder and a marvel that God has not cast me off; that He has not said to me, 'I will no more speak My Word through you. I will leave you to yourself; you shall be like Samson when his hair was gone.'"[188]

Spurgeon gives reason for his ministry despite personal unworthiness: "I know and am fully assured that I am justified by 'faith which is in Christ Jesus.' I am treated as if I had been perfectly just and made an heir of God and a joint-heir with

Christ. And yet by nature, I must take my place among the most sinful. Though altogether undeserving, I am treated as if I had been deserving. I am loved with as much love as if I had always been godly, whereas before I was ungodly. Who can help being astonished at this demonstration of grace? Gratitude for such favor stands dressed in robes of wonder."[189] Amen and amen.

Speaking to an audience of aspiring preachers, he said, "The best man here knows—if he knows what he is—that he is out of depth in his sacred calling."[190] In the sermon "Self Low, but Christ High," he states, "A sense of unworthiness is exceedingly useful, because it puts a man where God can bless him....Down with self, and up with Christ."[191] And in the sermon "Fresh Grace," he says, "If you are a minister of the gospel, you will have a thousand reasons for feeling yourself to be incompetent, and you might well throw down the staff of your pastorate and leave work, if you were not sure that your sufficiency is of God. In such work as the instruction of the young, the visitation of the sick, and the reclaiming of the fallen, or whatever it is that God has called you to, you will frequently tremble as you discover more and more your own unfitness to be used of God; but this will be counterbalanced by learning more and more the divine faithfulness."[192]

In the classic devotional "Morning and Evening" (originally separate volumes), Spurgeon wrote, "The more unworthy you feel yourself to be, the more evidence have you that nothing but unspeakable love could have led the Lord Jesus to save such a soul as yours. The more demerit you feel, the clearer is the display of the abounding love of God in having chosen you, and called you, and made you an heir of bliss."[193] Saith Paul, "God has chosen what is insignificant and despised in the world—what is viewed as nothing—to bring to nothing what is viewed as something" (1 Corinthians 1:28 CSB). Martin Lloyd-Jones writes, "The man who is called by

God is a man who realizes what he is called to do, and he so realizes the awfulness of the task that he shrinks from it."[194]

Timothy Keller writes, "The irony of the Gospel is that the only way to be worthy of it is to admit that you're completely unworthy of it."[195] Saith Reuen Thomas, "What preacher who does not at times, and sincerely, say within himself, *I am not worthy to be called a preacher.* But as Paul had to be an apostle, notwithstanding his self-deprecation, so you and I have to be that to which we are called, or deny the Christ of God as an all-sufficient Savior. It would be an act of deliberate disobedience if I, feeling my utter unworthiness to be a preacher of the Gospel, should yet refuse to do it when I am called, inasmuch as I believe, intellectually and heartily, that Jesus is God's Christ and came to be man's Redeemer and Savior."[196] And Hudson Taylor provides the unworthy preacher (such as we all are) with this encouragement: "All God's giants have been weak men who did great things for God because they reckoned on God being with them."[197]

4

The Preacher's Doubt

"Our ground of trust is not to be found in our experience, but in the person and work of our Lord Jesus."[198] ~ C. H. Spurgeon

Spurgeon acknowledged his personal struggle with doubting his salvation—a conflict that Paul never experienced (2 Timothy 1:12)—in the sermon "The Glorious Right Hand of the Lord." He states, "I must confess here, with sorrow, that I have seasons of despondency and depression of spirit, which I trust none of you are called to suffer, and at such times I have doubted my interest in Christ, my calling, my election, my perseverance, my Savior's blood, and my Father's love."[199]

And in the sermon "The Roaring Lion," he attests, "My peculiar temptation has been constant unbelief. I know that God's promise is true. Yet does this temptation incessantly assail me: 'Doubt Him; distrust Him; He will leave you yet.' I can assure you when that temptation is aided by a nervous state of mind, it is very hard to stand day by day and say, 'No, I cannot doubt my God.'"[200]

Further, in the sermon "The Believer Sinking in the Mire," he asserts, "Some of us who have preached the Word for years and have been the means of working faith in others and of establishing them in the knowledge of the fundamental doctrines of the Bible have nevertheless been the subjects of the most fearful and violent doubts as to the truth of the very Gospel we have preached. I dare say, many of you think that God's ministers never have any question about their interest in Jesus Christ. I wish they never had; brethren, I wish sincerely I never had. It is seldom that I do—very seldom; but there are times when I would change my soul's place with the meanest believer out of Heaven, when I should be content to sit behind the door of Heaven, if only I might be numbered among God's people."[201] Whatever your thoughts of Spurgeon, you have to admire his brutal honesty and transparency.

Spurgeon feared that doubt sometimes arises from salvation experience comparisons and addressed that matter in the sermon "Is Conversion Necessary?" Saith Spurgeon, "God's Spirit calls men to Jesus in divers ways. Some are drawn so gently that they scarce know when the drawing began, and others are so suddenly affected that their conversion stands out with noonday clearness. Perhaps no two conversions are precisely alike in detail; the means, the modes, the manifestations all vary greatly. As our minds are not cast in the same mold, it may so happen that the truth which affects one is powerless upon another; the style of address which influences your friend may be offensive to yourself, and that which leads him to decide may only cause you to delay. 'The wind bloweth where it listeth.' The Holy Ghost is called 'the free Spirit,' and in the diversity of His operations that freeness is clearly seen. Again and again have I warned you against imitating others in the matter of conversion, lest you be found counterfeits, and it is well when another voice unites with me in the warning. Yet in all true conversions there are points of essential agreement: there must be in all a penitent confession of sin and a looking to Jesus for the forgiveness of it, and there must also be a real change of heart such as shall affect the entire after life, and where these essential points are not to be found there is no genuine conversion."[202]

He continues, "There must be a time when a man ceases to be an unbeliever and becomes a believer in Jesus. I do not assert that it is necessary for us to know the day, but such a time there is. In many cases, however, the very day and hour and place are fully known."[203]

He likewise feared doubts resulting from reliance upon feelings and other subjective evidence instead of scriptural fact. Spurgeon says, "We can no more be saved by our feelings than by our works. 'Oh, but,' saith another, 'I have confidence that I am saved, for I have had a wonderful dream, and, moreover, I heard a voice, and saw a vision.' Rubbish all! Dreams, visions, voices! Throw them all away. There is not the slightest reliance to be placed upon them. 'What, not if I saw Christ?' No, certainly not, for vast multitudes saw Him in the days of His flesh, and died and perished after all. 'But surely a dream will save me.' It will give you a dreamy hope, and when you awake in the next world your dream will be gone."[204]

And doubting, the great preacher says, comes from neglect of prayer. He states, "Would you wish to hatch the egg of unbelief till it turns into a serpent? Restrain prayer! Would you see evils magnified and mercies diminished? Would you find your tribulations increased sevenfold and your faith diminished in proportion? Restrain prayer! I say unto thee this day, if thou wilt neglect thy closet, all the troubles thou hast ever had shall be as nothing compared with what will yet come upon thee. The little finger of thy future doubts shall be thicker than the loins of thy present mental anguish."[205]

Former sin may also cause doubt of salvation. Spurgeon counsels, "Thy sins trouble thee; but God has cast thy sins behind His back, and thou art accepted in the Righteous One. Thou hast to fight with corruption and to wrestle with temptation, but thou art already accepted in Him who has overcome the powers of evil. The Devil tempts thee. Be of good cheer; he cannot destroy thee, for thou art accepted in Him who has broken Satan's head. Know by full assurance thy glorious standing."[206]

What is the cure for "preacher's doubt"? In the sermon "Come, My Beloved!" he shares, "I have told you before that some years ago I felt a great depression of spirit; I knew whom I had believed, but somehow I could not get the comfort out of the truth I preached. I even began to wonder whether I was really saved; and, having a holiday and being away from home, I went to the Wesleyan Chapel, and a local preacher occupied the pulpit that morning. While he preached a sermon full of the Gospel, the tears flowed from my eyes and I was in such a perfect delirium of joy on hearing the Gospel, which I so seldom have an opportunity of doing, that I said, 'Oh, yes, there is spiritual life within me, for the Gospel can touch my heart, and stir my soul.'"[207] He found a cure in the hearing of the Gospel. "Faith cometh by hearing, and hearing by the Word of God" (Romans 10:17).

And a second help is shared in the sermon "The One Foundation." "The one thing to rest upon is the surer word of testimony: Christ Jesus came into the world to save sinners, and whosoever believeth in Him is not condemned. I believe in Him, and, therefore, I am not condemned. Why do I believe my sin to be forgiven? Because Jesus died to put away the sins of believers, and there is no condemnation to those who are in

Him. Why do I believe myself to be justified? Because he that believeth is justified; the word of God says so. How do I know that I am saved? Because Jesus Christ has declared that whosoever believeth in Him is not condemned. To believe in Him is to trust in Him, to make Him my foundation. I do trust in Him; He is my foundation, and I am saved, or else His word is not true. I know that His word is true, and therefore I am at rest. It is written, 'He that believeth in him hath everlasting life.' I believe in Him; therefore, I have everlasting life. I have His promise that I shall never perish, neither shall any pluck me out of His hand; therefore, I shall never perish, neither shall any separate me from His love. You see, then, there is no hope of salvation but what is fixed upon Christ alone; and I do invite and entreat you, if any of you have any hope which goes beyond Christ or beside Christ, get rid of it; throw it on a dunghill and loathe it as an insult to God."[208]

> Blessed assurance, Jesus is mine!
> Oh, what a foretaste of glory divine!
> Heir of salvation, purchase of God
> Born of his Spirit, washed in His blood.
>
> ~ Fanny Crosby (1873)

Spurgeon resolved his doubt. Do thou likewise. Why? Saith Spurgeon, "There is nothing that can make you strong to labor for God, bold to fight against your enemies, and mighty to resist your temptations like a full assurance that God is your God and your sure salvation. Your doubts and fears weaken you. A fully assured Christian is a very giant in our Israel; for happiness and beauty he standeth like Saul, head and shoulders taller than the rest; while for strength and courage he can match with David and is like the angel of the Lord."[209] Hear Spurgeon again on the matter: "I can understand a man doubting whether he is truly converted or not, but I cannot countenance his apathy in resting quiet till he has solved the riddle."[210]

Adrian Rogers offers additional help to the preacher struggling with assurance of salvation. "If you can't remember when you were saved, that's okay. I want to help you do what I did as a teenage boy many years ago. I turned to the Lord when I was faced with uncertainty. I said, 'God, I don't know whether I am lost and the Holy Spirit has me under conviction or whether I am saved and the Devil is trying to make me doubt it. But one thing I know: I want to get it certain right now. You said that if I would believe You, then You would save me. With all my heart, as much in me is, once and for all, now and forever, I trust You to save me."[211]

5
The Preacher's Slander

"Leave your character with God; it is safe there. Men may throw mud at it, but it will never stick long on a true believer; it shall soon come off and you shall be the more glorious for men's slander."[212] ~ C. H. Spurgeon

Paul was slanderously accused, among other things, of preaching that the more man sins, the more glory will redound to God (Romans 3:8). He was slandered by his opponents in Thessalonica (Acts 17) who agitated many against him out of jealousy. Spurgeon also was no stranger to slander. Besieged with malicious untruth and injurious verbal assault, he wrote in 1857, "Down on my knees have I often fallen, with the hot sweat rising from my brow under some fresh slander poured upon me; in an agony of grief my heart has been well-nigh broken....This thing I hope I can say from my heart: if to be made as the mire of the streets again, if to be the laughingstock of fools and the song of the drunkard once more will make me more serviceable to my Master and more useful to His cause, I will prefer it to all this multitude or to all the applause that man could give."[213] Further, he said, "They began to say all manner of evil against the preacher; but the more I stank in their nostrils the better I liked it, for the surer I was that I was really dead to the world."[214]

In *An All-Round Ministry* Spurgeon wrote, "Men cannot say anything worse of me than they have said. I have been belied from head to foot and misrepresented to the last degree. My good looks are gone, and none can damage me much now."[215] In the sermon "Heart's Ease" he said, "The more prominent you are in Christ's service, the more certain are you to be the butt of calumny [a false, defamatory statement]. I have long ago said farewell to my character. I lost it in the earlier days of my ministry by being a little more zealous than suited a slumbering age. And I have never been able to regain it except in the sight of Him who judges all the earth, and in the hearts of those who love me for my work's sake."[216] In the sermon "David's Five-Stringed Harp" he says, "Slander is like shooting at a man with only powder, or with very small shot that can sting but cannot kill."[217] "Falsehoods," he said, "usually carry their own refutation somewhere about them and sting themselves to death. Some lies especially have a peculiar smell, which betrays their rottenness to every honest nose. If you are disturbed by them, the object of their invention is partly answered, but your silent endurance disappoints malice and gives you a partial victory, which God in His care of you will soon turn into a complete deliverance."[218]

How did Paul and Spurgeon respond to vicious slander? Paul testifies, "When we are slandered [reputation attacked], we try to be conciliatory and answer softly" (1 Corinthians 4:13 AMP).

Spurgeon said, "We would say of the general gossip of the village, and of the unadvised words of angry friends—do not hear them; or if you must hear them, do not lay them to heart. If we are compelled to hear the hasty language, we must endeavor to obliterate it from the memory and say with David, 'But I, as a deaf man, heard not. I was as a man that heareth not, and in whose mouth are no reproofs'" (Psalm 38:13).[219]

In the sermon "My Times Are in Thy Hand" Spurgeon said, "It is impossible to stop malicious tongues. They wound, and even slay, the characters of the godly."[220]

What is the wisest course to take? Saith Spurgeon in *The Treasury of David,* "It is of little use to appeal to our fellows on the matter of slander, for the more we stir in it the more it spreads; it is of no avail to appeal to the honor of the slanderers, for they have none, and the most piteous demands for justice will only increase their malignity and encourage them to fresh insult. As well plead with panthers and wolves as with black hearted traducers. However, when cries to man would be our weakness, cries to God will be our strength. To whom should children cry but to their father? Does not some good come even out of that vile thing, falsehood, when it drives us to our knees and to our God?"[221] When slandered pray with the psalmist, "Let the lying lips be put to silence" (Psalm 31:18). Spurgeon comments, "May God silence them either by leading them to repentance, by putting them to thorough shame, or by placing them in positions where what they may say will stand for nothing."[222]

Further he advises not to retaliate, "since none can slander the slanderer; he is too black to be blackened. Neither would any of us blacken him if we could. Wretched being! He fights with weapons which true men cannot touch."[223]

And Spurgeon urges use of the shield of faith. He says, "Many are the fiery darts of the evil one, but our shield is one. Though the javelins of the foe were dipped in the venom of Hell, yet our one shield of faith would hold us harmless, casting them off from us."[224]

In the book "Eccentric Preachers" Spurgeon states, "True pastors have enough of care and travail without being burdened by undeserved and useless faultfinding. [Do I hear a hearty amen?] We have something better to do than to be ever answering every malignant or frivolous slander which is set afloat to injure us. The rougher and stronger among us laugh at those who ridicule us, but upon others the effect is very sorrowful."[225]

What is the minister's safe haven amidst slander? Sweet communion with the Lord. Saith Spurgeon, "When I was quite a young man, I was greatly reviled for preaching the Gospel; and, sometimes, my heart would sink a little under the cruel slanders that many uttered; but I used to often go upstairs to my room, and after a season of sweet fellowship with my Lord, I would come down singing."[226]

Relief from slander is found in knowing that God knows the truth. Spurgeon says, "The Lord knows the truth. Though you have been sadly misunderstood, if not willingly misrepresented by ungenerous persons, yet God knows all about you; and His knowledge is of more importance than the opinion of dying men."[227]

Relief is found in the companionship of Christ. In the sermon "The Unrivaled Friend" he states, "Some ill word has been spoken in which there was no truth, but it has sufficed to turn away the esteem of many; but your Lord has gone with you through shame and abuse, and never for a single moment has He even hinted that He only loved you because you were had in respect by men. Ever faithful, ever true has been this friend, who loveth at all times."[228]

> Though my soul is among lions, yet no lion can bite me while Jehovah's angel is my guard.
>
> C. H. Spurgeon

And relief is found in knowing that God is able to restrain man's lips. In the sermon "My Times are in Thy Hand" Spurgeon remarks of slanderers, "They cannot utter a single whisper more than God permits. Go on thy way, O righteous man, and let false tongues pour forth their poison as they will. 'Every tongue that shall rise against thee in judgment thou shalt condemn' (Isaiah 54:17). If my times are in God's hand, no man can do me harm unless God permit. Though my soul is among lions, yet no lion can bite me while Jehovah's angel is my guard."[229] God was faithful to keep the lions that assaulted him toothless, enabling him to say in 1879, "Having had more than my fair share of criticism and abuse, I am not one jot the worse for it in any respect; no bones are broken, my position is not injured, and my mind is not soured."[230]

Spurgeon's wife, Susannah, wrote, "The Lord knows all about us. Our enemies—sometimes, even our friends—misunderstand and malign us; they misconstrue our words and actions and impute to us motives which never actuated us. But our God knows the thoughts and intents of our heart and never makes a mistake in the judgment He passes on us. The comfort of this knowledge on the Lord's part to those who are 'suffering wrongly' is inexpressibly precious. They can lift up their heads with joy and say, 'The Lord is good. He knows those who trust in Him.' I have known this comfort to so delight my soul that trials and temptations had no power to vex or annoy it, for my soul was hidden 'secretly in a pavilion from *the strife of tongues.*'"[231]

Spurgeon gives a warning to which the minister ought to give heed: "Slander is an old-fashioned weapon out of the armory of Hell and is still in plentiful use; and no matter how holy a man may be, there will be some who will defame him."[232] When slandered, lean heavily upon the promise of God cited by the prophet Isaiah: "No weapon that is formed against thee shall prosper; and every tongue that shall rise against thee in judgment thou shalt condemn. This is the heritage of the servants of the LORD, and their righteousness is of me, saith the LORD" (Isaiah 54:17).

Expressing not only his fervent desire but that of every preacher, Spurgeon addressed the Lord in *Treasury of David,* saying, "Permit me to enjoy a sense of thy favor, O Lord, and a consciousness that Thou art pleased with my manner of life, and all men may frown and slander as they will."[233] In addition, he states, "It is always enough for a servant if he pleases his master; others may be dissatisfied, but he is not their servant, they do not pay him his wages, and their opinions have no weight with him."[234]

6
The Preacher's Criticism

"Every man needs a blind eye and a deaf ear, so when people applaud, you'll only hear half of it, and when people salute, you'll only see part of it. Believe only half the praise and half the criticism."[235] ~ C. H. Spurgeon

All preachers bear a target on their backs at which many take aim. Chuck Swindoll states, "One of the occupational hazards of being a leader is receiving criticism (not all of it constructive, by the way). In the face of that kind of heat, there's a strong temptation to 'go under,' 'throw in the towel,' 'bail out.' Many have faded out of leadership because of intense criticism. I firmly believe that the leader who does anything that is different or worthwhile or visionary can count on criticism."[236]

Paul quotes his critics, "For they say, 'His letters are weighty and strong, but his bodily presence is weak, and his speech contemptible'" (2 Corinthians 10:10 NRSV). Spurgeon was criticized by pastors and newspapers. The *Essex Standard* (April 1855 edition) stated of him, "His style is that of the vulgar colloquial, varied by rant....All the most solemn mysteries of our holy religion are by him rudely, roughly and impiously handled. Common sense is outraged and decency disgusted. His rantings are interspersed with coarse anecdotes." The Ipswich Express criticized Spurgeon's preaching as "redolent of bad taste, vulgar, and theatrical."[237]

Rev. James Wells, pastor of Surrey Tabernacle, cast doubt on Spurgeon's conversion in a Christian publication and warned that his followers were likely to being fatally deluded.[238] "Critics complained that his plainspoken, direct speaking style was too edgy—and dangerously innovative."[239] Helmut Thielicke said, "Such critics ought to see in this man Spurgeon the shepherd who was willing to allow his robe—including his clerical robe—to be torn to tatters by thorns and sharp stones as he clambered after the lost sheep....Worldly preaching is impossible without having the earth leave its traces on a man's wardrobe. Here there are no robes that look as if they had just come out of a sandbox."[240]

"Paul was as indifferent to criticism," says R. G. Lee, "as he was stubborn for righteousness."[241] See 1 Corinthians 13:5. Spurgeon, likewise not easily jarred by criticism, said, "Public men must expect public criticism."[242] "You must," he writes, "be able to bear criticism, or you are not fit to be at the head of the congregation; and you must let the critic go without reckoning him among your deadly foes, or you will prove yourself a mere weakling."[243] Jesus said, "Woe unto you, when all men speak well of you! for so did their fathers to the false prophets" (Luke 6:26).

Saith Leonard Ravenhill, "If you stir Hell up, the Devil will stir everything he can against you; you'll get misunderstood, misrepresented....if you're not mature enough, it will get you down. It's not the contradiction of sinners....It's the criticism of saints that gets you down."[244] Thin-skinned preachers must toughen up. Vance Havner asserted, "A preacher should have the mind of a scholar, the heart of a child and the hide of a rhinoceros. His biggest problem is how to toughen his hide without hardening his heart."[245]

How might the hide of the preacher be toughened while the heart remains tender? "Just pray," says Ruth Graham, "for a tough hide and a tender heart."[246] Spurgeon's sensitivity toughened over time to the point he could say, "If all the sages of the world were to utter one thundering sarcasm, if they concentrated all their scorn into one universal sneer of contempt, I do not think it would now affect me the turn of a hair, so sure am I that my Lord will justify my confidence."[247] In his autobiography, Spurgeon remarked, "However much I may now be misrepresented, it will one day be known that I have honestly striven for the glory of my Master."[248]

However much I may now be misrepresented, it will one day be known that I have honestly striven for the glory of my Master.

Charles Spurgeon

What is the preacher's response to criticism? Ignore it if it's counted as destructive. Solomon advises, "Do not take to heart *all* the things that people say" (Ecclesiastes 7:21 ESV) and "ignore an insult" (Proverbs 12:16 GNT). Spurgeon said, "If we dwell on high with 'that great Shepherd of the sheep' we shall care little for all the confused bleatings around us, but if we become 'carnal, and walk as men,' we shall have little rest if we listen to this, that, and the other which every poor sheep may bleat about us."[249]

Give it a deaf ear and a blind eye (as Spurgeon would say). Don't rush to defend yourself. "Be slow to speak" (James 1:19 NIRV). Spurgeon advises, "In almost all cases, it is the wisest course to let such things die a natural death. A great lie, if unnoticed, is like a big fish out of water—it dashes and plunges and beats itself to death in a short time. Our best course is to defend our innocence by our silence and leave our reputation with God. Yet there are exceptions to this general rule. When distinct, definite, public charges are made against a man, he is bound to answer them, and answer them in the clearest and most open manner."[250] Spurgeon said, "Your blameless life will be your best defense and those that have seen it will not allow you to be condemned so readily as your slanderers expect."[251] Saith Plato, "When men speak ill of thee, live so as nobody may believe them."

Hold firm to the promises. At a time when Spurgeon's resilience to criticism waned (an uncommon occurrence) his wife, seeing its effect, intervened. She printed the words of Matthew 5:10–12 onto a large piece of paper and hung it on the ceiling above the side of the bed where he slept. "Blessed are those who have been persecuted for the sake of righteousness, for theirs is the kingdom of heaven. Blessed are you when people insult you and persecute you, and falsely say all kinds of evil against you because of Me. Rejoice and be glad, for your reward in heaven is great; for in the same way they persecuted the prophets who were before you" (Matthew 5:10–12 NASB). These words of Jesus remained fastened on the ceiling giving him encouragement morning and night until his resilience against criticism was restored.

Likewise, when criticism becomes heartwrenching, rest in the promise of God (Psalm 91:14–16), and don't live in suspicion of it. Saith Spurgeon, "Suspicion in kings creates tyranny, in husbands jealously, and in ministers bitterness—such bitterness as in spirit dissolves all the ties of the pastoral relation, eating like a corrosive acid into the very soul of the office, and making it a curse rather than a blessing."[252]

The bottom line with regard to destructive and unjust criticism is stated in an Arabian proverb: "The dogs bark but the caravan moves on." Spurgeon and Paul heard a lot of barking dogs, but their ministries were never impeded by them.

Note, constructive criticism given from a heart of love is an opportunity to change and improve your ministry. Spurgeon, when preaching at Surry Gardens, had an unknown critic that sent him a weekly list of his mispronunciations and other speech mistakes. Of him, he states, "Possibly some young men might have been discouraged, if not irritated, by such severe criticisms, but they would have been very foolish, for in resenting such correction, they would have been throwing away a valuable aid to progress."[253]

Theodore Roosevelt, in the speech entitled "Citizenship in a Republic" (April 23, 1910), stated, "It is not the critic who counts, not the man who points out how the strong man stumbles or where the doer of deeds could have done them better. The credit belongs to the man who is actually in the arena; whose face is marred by dust and sweat and blood; who strives valiantly; who errs; who comes short again and again, because there is no effort without error and shortcoming, but who does actually strive to do the deeds; who knows great enthusiasms, the great devotions; who spends himself in a worthy cause; who at the best knows in the end the triumph of high achievement, and who at the worst, if he fails, at least fails while daring greatly, so that his place shall never be with those cold and timid souls who neither know victory nor defeat."

7
The Preacher's Loneliness

"More or less, we must be alone in the service of God. Christian companionship is a great comfort, but if a man becomes a leader in Israel, he becomes a lonely spirit to a certain degree."[254] ~ C. H. Spurgeon

Research states that sixty-one percent of pastors are lonely. Paul experienced the pain of loneliness. He said, "This thou knowest, that all they which are in Asia be turned away from me; of whom are Phygellus and Hermogenes." "At my first answer no man stood with me, but all men forsook me" (2 Timothy 1:15; 4:16).

Spurgeon, though the most popular of preachers in his day, battled loneliness. He wrote, "This loneliness, which if I mistake not is felt by many of my brethren, is a fertile source of depression."[255] Speaking to aspiring preachers at the Pastors' College he said, "A minister fully equipped for his work will usually be a spirit by himself, above, beyond, and apart from others. The most loving of his people cannot enter into his peculiar thoughts, cares, and temptations. In the ranks, men walk shoulder to shoulder with many comrades, but as the officer rises in rank, men of his standing are fewer in number. There are many soldiers, few captains, fewer colonels, but only one commander-in-chief. So, in our churches, the man whom the Lord raises as a leader becomes, in the same degree in which he is a superior man, a solitary man. The mountaintops stand solemnly apart and talk only with God as he visits their terrible solitudes."[256]

Isolation in ministry is a surefire path to loneliness. Make room on your plate to cultivate friendships with preachers of like mind and belief. Even the Lone Ranger had his Tonto. No one understands a preacher like another preacher. Saith Spurgeon: "Our ministers' fraternal meeting and the cultivation of holy intercourse with kindred minds will with God's blessing help us greatly to escape the snare [loneliness]."[257]

Paul nor Spurgeon tackled ministry alone. Paul's companions included Barnabas, Silas, Timothy, Epaphroditus; and Spurgeon's, George Müller, Earl of Shaftesbury, W. Y. Fullerton, John Ruskin, and William Harrald. Note, at the death of Spurgeon, January 31, 1891, the deacons of the Metropolitan Tabernacle sent a telegram to William Harrald, Spurgeon's personal secretary, which read, "Among the most faithful of the faithful friends of our beloved pastor, you are the most faithful of faithful friends."[258] What an honorable compliment!

Spurgeon said, "Friendship is one of the sweetest joys of life. Many might have failed beneath the bitterness of their trial had they not found a friend." (Doubtlessly Spurgeon spoke from experience.) May every pastor be blessed with a friend like William Harrald who will uphold him in the most difficult seasons of ministry and life.

Though alone, the preacher is not really alone. Saith Spurgeon, "Yet we shall not be alone, my brethren. The Father will be with us; Jesus will be with us; the eternal Comforter will be with us; the everlasting Godhead in the Trinity of persons shall be with us, and the angels of God shall be our convoy."[259]

8
The Preacher's Ridicule

"Ridicule is always hard to bear, but when we are in intense pain, it is so heartless, so cruel, that it cuts us to the quick."[260] ~ C. H. Spurgeon

Saith Spurgeon, "Mockery was a great ingredient in our Lord's woe. Judas mocked Him in the garden, the chief priests and scribes laughed Him to scorn, Herod set Him at naught, the servants and the soldiers jeered at Him and brutally insulted Him, Pilate and his guards ridiculed His royalty, and on the tree all sorts of horrid jests and hideous taunts were hurled at Him."[261] And Jesus said, "The servant is not greater than his lord; neither he that is sent greater than he that sent him" (John 13:16). In other words, ridicule comes with the territory for Christ's servant.

Spurgeon gives testimony of a time of ridicule: "When I was exceedingly ill in the South of France and deeply depressed in spirit—so deeply depressed and so sick and ill that I scarcely knew how to live—one of those malicious persons who commonly haunt all public men and especially ministers sent me anonymously a letter, openly directed to 'That unprofitable servant, C. H. Spurgeon.' This letter contained tracts directed to the enemies of the Lord Jesus, with passages marked and underlined—with notes applying them to myself. How many 'Rabshakehs'—liars, ridiculers, blasphemers (Isaiah 36:4–21)—have, in their day, written to me! Ordinarily I read them with the patience which comes of use and they go to light the fire. I do not look for exemption from this annoyance, nor do I usually feel it hard to bear, but in the hour when my spirits were depressed and I was in terrible pain, this reviling letter cut me to the quick. I turned upon my bed and asked, *Am I, then, an unprofitable servant?* I grieved exceedingly and could not lift up my head or find rest. I reviewed my life and saw its infirmities and imperfections, but knew not how to put my case till this second text [Luke 17:10] came to my relief and answered as the verdict of my bruised heart. I said to myself, *I hope I am not an unprofitable servant in the sense in which this person intends to call me so, but I am assuredly so in the other sense.* I cast myself upon my Lord and Master once again with a deeper sense of the meaning of the text than I had felt before. His atoning Sacrifice revived me and in humble faith I found rest."[262]

And a newspaper wrote of Spurgeon that he "is a nine-days' wonder, a comet that has suddenly shot across the religious atmosphere. He has gone up like a rocket, and ere long will come down like a stick."[263] Saith Spurgeon, "Be ready for a bad name; be willing to be called a bigot; be prepared for loss of friendships; be prepared for anything so long as you can stand fast by Him who bought you with His precious blood. God give you courage, more and more of it, through faith in Himself! May you be willing to put your religion to every proper test, the test of life, and the test of death, too!"[264]

Paul also knew ridicule. He was laughed and sneered upon for preaching about the resurrection of the dead (Acts 17:32). Henry Ward Beecher said, "Some men are, in regard to ridicule, like tin-roofed buildings in regard to hail: all that hits them bounds rattling off; not a stone goes through."[265]

May that be so with the man of God. Saith Spurgeon, "You cannot stop people's tongues, and therefore the best thing is to stop your own ears and never mind what is spoken."[266]

> You cannot stop people's tongues, and therefore the best thing is to stop your own ears and never mind what is spoken.
>
> Charles Spurgeon

9
The Preacher's Bodily Suffering

"To shed tears and yet to sow! To be racked with pain and to turn the couch into a pulpit!"[267] ~ C. H. Spurgeon

Suffering prepares God's man for God's assignment. A. W. Tozer said, "It is doubtful whether God can bless a man greatly until He has hurt him deeply."[268] Both Paul and Spurgeon illustrate that premise. Chuck Swindoll states, "History proves that struggles and scars pave the way for remarkable achievements."[269]

Paul was afflicted with a thorn (thought to be a physical infirmity) throughout his ministry. But sufficient grace was supplied to enable him to endure it and continue his ministry (2 Corinthians 12:7). Spurgeon told his congregation, "Do not think it unspiritual to remember that you have a body. The physician is often as needful as the minister."[270] And in the sermon "A Homily For Humble Folks," he states, "The troubled man experiences a good deal, not because he is a Christian, but because he is a man, a sickly man, a man inclined to melancholy."[271] In the sermon "My Times are in Thy Hand," Spurgeon said, "I have not been able to preach on this text as I hoped to do, for I am full of pain."[272]

From the age of thirty-three he lived in pain caused by gout, rheumatism, neuritis, and burning kidney inflammation (Blight Disease). These health issues progressively grew worse so that "approximately one-third of the last twenty-two years of his ministry was spent out of the Tabernacle pulpit, either suffering, or convalescing, or taking precautions against the return of illness."[273] Tom Nettles, in his biography of Spurgeon, called him "a living theology of suffering."[274]

Spurgeon, like Paul with his suffering, refused to quit. Saith Spurgeon, "God works all things together for your good. If the waves roll against you, it only speeds your ship towards the port."[275] "The worst days I have ever had have turned out to be my best days, and when God has seemed most cruel to me, He has then been most kind. If there is anything in this world for which I would bless Him more than for anything else, it is for pain and affliction. I am sure that in these things the richest, tenderest love has been manifested to me."[276]

F. W. Robertson (English minister) experienced sleepless nights and torture-filled days with pain in the back of the head and neck that made life dreadful to him. Often, he would clench his teeth to prevent cries of pain.[277] Robert Hall (English Baptist minister) lived in such pain that often he would roll on the carpet in agony over the pain in his back. Fittingly, the inscription on his tomb reads, "Neither shall there be any more pain."[278] George W. Truett (pastor of the First Baptist Church, Dallas, Texas, for 47 years) suffered from an agonizing illness an entire year prior to death. With Paul, Spurgeon, these men, and myriads of others like them you may well identify: torturing, unrelenting tortuous pain is your lot in life.

Chuck Swindoll said of pain, "It communicates its own message, whether to statesman or servant, preacher or prodigal, mother or child."[279] And no one can understand it except the one who bears it. Pain has a designed purpose. Timothy Keller states, "There is a purpose to it, and if faced rightly, it can drive us like a nail deep into the love of God and into more stability and spiritual power than you can imagine."[280] Spurgeon testified, "I am certain that I never did grow in grace one-half so much anywhere as I have upon the bed of pain."[281]

Suffering intersects with effective ministry according to Spurgeon. In the 1876 edition of the *Sword and Trowel,* he wrote, "It is good for a man to bear the yoke of service, and he is no loser when it is exchanged for the yoke of suffering. May not severe discipline fall to the lot of some to qualify them for their office of under-shepherds? How can we speak with consoling authority to a situation which we have never known? *The complete pastor's life will be an epitome* of the lives of his people, and they will turn to his preaching as men do to David's psalms, to see themselves and their sorrows, as in a mirror. Their needs will be the reason for his griefs. As in the case of the Lord himself, perfect equipment for his work came only through suffering, and so must it be for those who are called to follow him in binding up the brokenhearted and loosing the prisoners."[282]

In the sermon "Cheer Up, My Comrades!" Spurgeon states, "You are ill; the vigor you felt in the bright days of health fails you now; you have to suffer pain, weariness, and exhaustion; you are often detained at home; and home seems now to you a gloomy hospital all the day long rather than a genial hostelry when evening shadows fall. Little indeed, therefore, can you do—so little that you are apt to reckon it as nothing at all. The thought is a burden to you. You wish you could serve the Lord. How constantly you have dreamed of the pleasure since you have been denied the privilege! How willing your feet would be to run; how ready your hands would be to labor; how glad would your tongue be to testify! You envy those who are able, and you would fain emulate and excel them; not indeed that you harbor ill-will against them, but you devoutly wish that you could do some personal service in the cause of your Master."[283]

The final Christmas letter John R. Rice wrote (December 1980) vividly portrays the restrictive power of the chain of illness. He dreamed of preaching and soul winning, but the chains of infirmity hindered him.

"I still, from my armchair, preach in great revival campaigns. I still envision hundreds walking the aisles to accept Christ. I still feel hot tears for the lost. I still see God working miracles. Oh, how I long to see great revivals, to hear about revival crowds once again! I want no Christmas without a burden for lost souls, a message for sinners, a heart to bring in the lost sheep so dear to the Shepherd, the sinning souls for whom Christ died. May food be tasteless and music a discord and Christmas a farce if I forget the dying millions to whom I am debtor, if this fire in my bones does not still flame! Not till I die or not till Jesus comes will I ever be eased of this burden, these tears, this toil to save souls."[284]

If you find yourself in such a dismal place, be encouraged in knowing that Christ has enacted David's law of just recompense for all His soldiers. Soldiers in David's army inapt for battle who therefore remained at the camp in the trenches to guard the supplies shared equally in the bounty recovered by the men in the fray of battle. "As his part is that goeth down to the battle, so shall his part be that tarrieth by the stuff: they shall part alike. And it was so from that day forward, that he made it a statute and an ordinance for Israel" (1 Samuel 30:24–25).

Spurgeon says that Jesus' law is no less gracious. "If by sickness you are detained at home, if for any other reason, such as age or infirmity, you are not able to enter into actual service, yet if you are a true soldier and would fight if you could, and your heart is in it, you shall share even with the best and bravest of those who, clad in the panoply of God, encounter and grapple with the adversary."[285]

If healthy and fully mobile, use the time wisely. Spurgeon advised, "If I have any message to give from my own bed of sickness, it would be this: if you do not wish to be full of regrets when you are obliged to lie still, work while you can. If you desire to make a sick bed as soft as it can be, do not stuff it with the mournful reflection that you wasted time while you were in health and strength."[286]

10
The Preacher's Persecution

"We are foolish to expect to serve God without opposition: the more zealous we are, the more sure are we to be assailed."[287] ~ C. H. Spurgeon

Paul was stoned in Lystra and dragged out of the city (Acts 14:19), imprisoned (2 Corinthians 11:23), beaten five times with thirty-nine whips (2 Corinthians 11:24), and far more. Paul, despite chains that bound him, preached the Gospel and penned three epistles (Ephesians, Philippians, Colossians) and one letter (Philemon). He could have easily given up. But he didn't. He resolved to extend his prison chain to its furthest extent of usefulness for Christ. Spurgeon states, "The world thinks as little of Paul as Paul does of the world. The world says, 'Oh, that harebrained Paul! He was once sensible, but he has gone mad upon that stubborn notion about the Crucified One! The man is a fool.' So, the world crucifies him."[288]

Saith Spurgeon, "If persecution should arise, you should be willing to part with all that you possess—with your liberty, with your life itself—for Christ, or you cannot be his disciple."[289] "Endure whatever you have to endure with the greatest possible meekness."[290]

This Spurgeon practiced. *The Daily News* accused him of "pulpit buffoonery and an utter ignorance of theology." *The Saturday Review* called him "a course, stupid, irrational bigot." Spurgeon's stance against slavery angered southerners in America that erupted upon his invitation to preach at the Academy Music Opera House in New York (an invitation he did not accept).

Christian George states, "Anti-Spurgeon bonfires illuminated jail yards, plantations, bookstores, and courthouses throughout the Southern states."[291] In protest to Spurgeon, the abolitionist people of Montgomery, Alabama, gathered to burn his "dangerous books." *The Southern Reporter and Daily Commercial Courier* quote a participant of that incident: "Last Saturday, we devoted to the flames a large number of copies of Spurgeon's sermons. We trust that the works of the greasy cockney vociferator ["one who cries out loudly and vehemently, especially in protest"[292]] may receive the same treatment throughout the South. And if the pharisaical author should ever show himself in these parts, we trust that a stout cord may speedily find its way around his eloquent throat."[293]

Among his greatest persecutors were Southern Baptists in America. Note, in 1873 Spurgeon invited the Fisk Jubilee Singers, an a cappella group composed of many former slaves from Tennessee, to the Tabernacle. Proceeds from the 10,000 in attendance helped finance Jubilee Hall, the first permanent building for what is now Fisk University in the USA.[294]

George Kulp wrote, "The preacher determined to go with God will find all Hell arranged against him, and in alliance with these worldly preachers and worldly church members. The more loyal he is to God, and the more faithful he is to his calling, the more he will be opposed. 'Marvel not if the world hate you, it hated me before it hated you,' Jesus said to His disciples."[295]

J. C. Ryle said, "Laughter, ridicule, opposition and persecution are often the only reward which Christ's followers get from the world."[296] Spurgeon counsels, "It is lawful to desire escape from persecution if it be the Lord's will; and when this may not be granted us in the form which we desire, sustaining grace will give us deliverance in another form, by enabling us to laugh to scorn all the fury of the foe."[297]

Spurgeon asserts, "To forsake the Lord through persecution is to set time before eternity, to barter Heaven for this world's pleasures, to renounce eternal life for a few hours of ease, and to involve ourselves in endless misery rather than endure a stupid jest or a senseless jibe. It comes to that."[298] In the sermon "The Scales of Judgment," Spurgeon forthrightly states that God will avenge him that is persecuted. There is no cause to retaliate. He says, "There has never been a deed of persecution—there has never been a drop of martyr's blood shed yet, but shall be avenged, and every land guilty of it shall yet drink the cup of the wine of the wrath of God."[299]

11
The Preacher's Betrayal

"It is a terrible wounding when he who should have been your friend becomes your foe, and when, like your Lord, you also have your Judas Iscariot. It is not easy to bear misrepresentation and falsehood, to have your purest motives misjudged. This is a very painful kind of wounded spirit."[300] ~ C. H. Spurgeon

Paul and Spurgeon did. False friends and believers sought Paul's undoing and failure (2 Corinthians 11:26). And Spurgeon wrote in a letter to a friend, "I have suffered enough for one lifetime from those I lived to serve."[301] Spurgeon's own brother, James, seconded the vote to censure him from the Baptist Union on April 23, 1888. That betrayal led

Spurgeon to say, "I feel heartbroken. Certainly, he has done the very opposite of what I should have done."[302]

Prepare for when your dearest
brother [friend] betrays you.
Charles Spurgeon

Saith Spurgeon, "An unkind word from a stranger may have a very slight effect upon us; but if such a word should come from the lips of one whom we love, it would cut us to the quick. We could put up with a thousand things from those who are mere acquaintances; but from a beloved child, or from the wife of our bosom [or friend] such a thing would be very hard to bear."[303] Addressing students at the Pastors' College he said, "The trials of a true minister are not few, and such as are caused by ungrateful professors are harder to bear than the coarsest attacks of avowed enemies."[304] Therefore, he advises, "Prepare for when your dearest brother [friend] betrays you." Calvin says, "Against a known foe we are on our watch, but the unsuspected stroke of a friend takes us by surprise."[305]

Nehemiah was betrayed by one considered to be a "godly" man, a priest, for material gain (Nehemiah 6:10–13). Delilah betrayed Samson to the Philistines (Judges 16:16–21) for the same reason. David betrayed Uriah to conceal his sin (2 Samuel 11:14–15); Absalom betrayed his father King David in an effort to steal the kingdom (2 Samuel 15:10–17); Haman betrayed the King and God's people in an effort to eradicate the Jews (Esther 3:8–11); Zedekiah the king betrayed Jeremiah in not protecting him against the princes' desire to kill him (Jeremiah 38:5); Peter betrayed Jesus for fear of persecution (John 18:15–27) and Jesus was betrayed by Judas to the Roman Guard (Matthew 26:15). David was the victim of betrayal by a servant of King Saul, Doeg the Edomite (Psalm

52), the Ziphites (Psalm 54), and by an intimate friend named Ahithophel (2 Samuel 15:31) which he addresses in Psalm 55.

Alexander Maclaren remarks on Psalm 55:12–14: "The psalmist feels that the defection of his false friend is the worst blow of all. He could have braced himself to bear an enemy's reviling; he could have found weapons to repel, or a shelter in which to escape from, open foes; but the baseness which forgets all former sweet companionship in secret, and all association in public and in worship, is more than he can bear up against. The voice of wounded love is too plain in the words for the hypothesis that the singer is the personified nation."[306] Saith Spurgeon, "We can bear from Shimei what we cannot endure from Ahithophel."[307]

How should we respond to betrayal?

1. Put your confidence in God. Saith Spurgeon, "Be prepared for anything so long as you can stand fast by Him who bought you with His precious blood."[308] And in the sermon "A Sacred Solo," he said, "It is frightfully easy for the heart to rely upon man, as we know right well! Confidence in man will betray your hopes, but faith in God will enrich you beyond your expectations."[309]

2. Take the high road. Gracefully confront the betrayer. Choke down the desire to get even, remembering the words of Paul: "Never take your own revenge, beloved, but leave room for the wrath of God, for it is written, 'VENGEANCE IS MINE, I WILL REPAY,' says the Lord" (Romans 12:9 NASB). Matthew Henry suggests, "We must refer ourselves to God and leave it to Him to plead our cause, to maintain our right, and reckon with those that do us wrong in such a way and manner as He thinks fit and in His own due time."[310]

3. Exhibit forgiveness. In the Lord's Prayer, Jesus assumes such forgiveness will be extended when we ask for His (Matthew 6:12). William Blake said, "It is easier to forgive an enemy than to forgive a friend."[311]

4. Don't harbor bitterness. "Bitterness will affect you physically, emotionally, and spiritually," declares Adrian Rogers, "because the fruit of bitterness is an acid that destroys its container."[312] "The Bible warns," states Jim Henry, "that the root of bitterness will spring up, and when it does, what does it do? Cause good things to happen? No! Cause joy? No! Cause love? No! Cause peace? No! 'See to it...that no bitter root grows up to cause trouble!'"[313]

5. Don't allow your hurts to turn into hates.[314]

6. Be ready to part ways. Betrayal may lead to the parting of ways. Remember, for every Shemaiah, Judas, Absalom, or Delilah that has betrayed you there is at least one Jonathan who may be trusted with your life. Don't rob yourself of the healing and help a Jonathan is willing and able to provide by locking him out of your life.

7. Move on with your ministry. Paul's betrayals didn't prevent him from 'keeping nothing back' (Acts 20:20). He gave his best to the work. And the same may be said of Spurgeon.

Note, man's betrayal, painful as it may be, will not thwart God's purpose for you. Judas' betrayal of Jesus didn't undermine God's divine plan with Jesus, nor did Joseph's brothers' betrayal of him undermine God's plan for him. God has a way of causing a betrayal to work for good (Romans 8:28). Spurgeon says, "Cruel slander, wicked misrepresentation, desertion of friends, betrayal by the most trusted one, and whatever else may come cannot hinder the LORD's purpose concerning you. The LORD stands by you in the night of your sorrow, and He says, 'Thou must yet bear witness for me.' Be calm; be filled with joy in the LORD."[315]

At the end of the war, upon visiting a lady at her home, General Robert E. Lee was shown the remains of a huge tree. She informed Lee with tears that the limbs of the tree were destroyed by Federal artillery fire and its trunk defaced by the

Union Army. The tree was like a family heirloom and just looking at it stirred bitter memories in her heart. The lady inquired of Lee as to what she should do about the tree. Lee said, "Cut it down, my dear Madam, and forget it."[316] The same applies to a betrayal that has sown the poisonous seed of bitterness in the heart. You have to "cut it down," letting go of that which has been eating away at you, and forget it by the grace of God.

12
The Preacher's Heaviness

"On the surface there is a stream of heaviness rolling with dark waves; but down in the depths there is a strong under-current of great rejoicing that is always flowing there."[317] ~ C. H. Spurgeon

Heaviness of heart is a sad, miserable or unhappy state that results from death, disappointment, defeat, desertion, or defamation. It may evolve into depression. In Asia, Paul was "weighed down exceedingly" (2 Corinthians 1:8 ASV). Spurgeon was frequently "in heaviness."[318] When in his early twenties, he experienced a traumatic event that crushed him beyond measure. A fire developed and pandemonium broke loose at the Royal Surrey Gardens Music Hall prior to his sermon (October 19, 1856). Seven people died and twenty-eight were hospitalized. Writing of that night he said, "Perhaps never a soul went so near the burning furnace of insanity, and yet came away unharmed."[319] Spurgeon's wife, Susannah, wrote of his mental state following that experience: "My beloved's anguish was so deep and violent that reason seemed to totter in her throne, and we sometimes feared that he would never preach again."[320]

Pastor W. Williams, a close friend to Spurgeon, in *Personal Reminiscences of Charles Hadden Spurgeon* gave a comment about the tragedy: "I cannot but think, from what I saw, that his comparatively early death might be in some measure due to the furnace of mental suffering he endured on and after that fearful night."[321] Contributing to the heaviness Spurgeon experienced were the antagonistic attacks of his enemies and the illness of Susannah, who in 1865 (age thirty-three) became a virtual invalid who seldom, thereafter, was able to travel with him for ministry purposes or even hear him preach.

Saith Spurgeon, "More than at any other time a man needs his God is when his heart is melted within him because of heaviness. Our souls may sometimes long and faint, and thirst even to the point of anguish, to see the light of the Lord's face; at such times let us calm ourselves by focusing on the sympathy of our great High Priest. Our drops of sorrow may be forgotten in the ocean of His griefs; how high ought our love to rise!"[322] Thus he would pray, as we ought in times of heaviness of soul, "O strong and deep love of Jesus, come in like a flood, cover all my powers, drown all my sins, wash away all my cares, lift up my earthbound soul, and bring me up to my Lord's feet."[323]

13
The Preacher's Depression

"Irons around the wrists can be worn till they fit easily; but when the iron enters into the soul, how it rusts the heart and eats into the spirit!"[324] ~ C. H. Spurgeon

Warren Wiersbe observed, "Depression and discouragement are occupational hazards of the ministry." Susannah Spurgeon wrote, "Depression of spirit is frequently the outcome of oppression of the flesh. Satan, ever on the alert to vex, if he cannot harm us, takes advantage of our sad condition to insinuate doubts and fears which we should not tolerate when in vigorous health."[325] Depression doesn't discriminate.

Even Paul knew what it was to be in complete despair (utterly hopeless) and 'burdened beyond strength' (2 Corinthians 1:8).

> I feel as if I had rather die than live; all that God hath done by me seems to be forgotten.
>
> Charles Spurgeon

Spurgeon, the Prince of Preachers, suffered episodes of deep depression throughout his ministry. In the introduction to the sermon "Fear Not," he said to his congregation, "I have to speak today to myself [sometimes every preacher has to do that], and while I shall be endeavoring to encourage those who are distressed and downhearted, I shall be preaching, I trust, to myself, for I need something which shall cheer my heart—why I cannot tell; wherefore I do not know, but I have a thorn in the flesh, a messenger of Satan to buffet me. My soul is cast down within me; I feel as if I had rather die than live. All that God hath done by me seems to be forgotten….I need your prayers. I need God's Holy Spirit, and I felt that I could not preach today unless I should preach in such a way as to encourage you and to encourage myself in the good work and labor of the Lord Jesus Christ."[326] In the sermon "The Upper Hand," he declared, "I do not suppose there is any person in this assembly who ever has stronger fits of depression of spirits than I have myself personally."[327]

Depression episodes were so painful that at times he would cry without knowing the reason ("causeless depression"[328]). He said, "I could weep by the hour like a child, and yet I knew not what I wept for."[329] He sought medical help from doctors (the depression they speculated was the result of "extra pressure of care or labor"[330]) and in over thirty books he owned on mental health, realizing it wasn't a spiritual problem. ("Some are touched with melancholy from their birth."[331])

In the sermon "Sweet Stimulants for the Fainting Soul," he says, "Depression of spirit is no index of declining Grace—the very loss of joy and the absence of assurance may be accompanied by the greatest advancement in the spiritual life."[332] And in the sermon "The Valley of the Shadow of Death," he says, "No sin is necessarily connected with sorrow of heart, for Jesus Christ our Lord once said, 'My soul is exceedingly sorrowful, even to death.' There was no sin in Him, and consequently none in His deep depression."[333]

In the sermon "Israel's God and God's Israel," he said, "I suppose that some brethren neither have much elevation or depression. I could almost wish to share their peaceful life. For I am much tossed up and down, and although my joy is greater than the most of men, my depression of spirit is such as few can have an idea of. I could say with Job, 'My soul chooseth strangling rather than life' (Job 7:15). I could readily enough have laid violent hands upon myself to escape from my misery of spirit."[334] In the sermon "The Saddest Cry from the Cross," he said, "Quite involuntarily, unhappiness of mind, depression of spirit, and sorrow of heart will come upon you. You may be without any real reason for grief, and yet may become among the most unhappy of men."[335] And in the sermon "The Frail Leaf," he said, "You may be surrounded with all the comforts of life and yet be in wretchedness more gloomy than death if the spirits are depressed. You may have no outward cause whatever for sorrow, and yet if the mind is dejected, the brightest sunshine will not relieve your gloom. There are times when all our evidences get clouded and all our joys are fled. Though we may still cling to the Cross, yet it is with a desperate grasp."[336]

Expressing depression's torment and pain, he said, "I think it would have been less painful to have been burned alive at the stake than to have passed through those horrors and depressions of spirit."[337] "I know of no life that has more trouble in it, I know of no occupation that brings more awful despondency of spirit on a man's mind than my ministry brings on me."[338] "The worst cloud of all is deep depression of spirit." "The worst ill in the world is a depressed spirit." "Of all things in the world to be, dreaded despair is the chief." "Depression is…the shadow of death." "Depression is…my horror of great darkness."[339]

Lecturing to his students on a needful subject, "The Minister's Fainting Fits," he said, "Knowing by most painful experience what deep depression of spirit means, being visited therewith at seasons by no means few or far between, I thought it might be consolatory to some of my brethren if I gave my thoughts thereon, that younger men might not fancy that some strange thing had happened to them when they became for a season possessed by melancholy, and that sadder men might know that one upon whom the sun has shone right joyously did not always walk in the light."[340] The pastor, says Spurgeon, is most vulnerable to depression because he bears the weight of lost souls, and the coldness of the godly, and witnesses the sinner's boldness in sin.[341]

"Sometimes you cannot raise your poor depressed spirits," he said. "Some say to you, 'Oh! you should not feel like this.' They tell you, 'Oh! you should not speak such words nor think such thoughts.' Ah! 'The heart knoweth its own bitterness, and a stranger intermeddleth not therewith,'—aye, and I will improve upon it: 'nor a friend either.' It is not easy to tell how another ought to feel and how another ought to act. Our minds are differently made, each in its own mold, which mold is broken afterwards, and there shall never be another like it. We are all different, each one of us; but I am sure there is one thing in which we are all brought to unite in times of deep sorrow; namely, in a sense of helplessness."[342]

In the sermon "The Saddest Cry from the Cross," Spurgeon urged patience and understanding with the depressed: "Some strong-minded people are very apt to be hard upon nervous folk and to say, 'They should not get into that state.' And we are liable to speak harshly to people who are very depressed in spirit and to say to them, 'Really, you ought to rouse yourself out of such a state.' I hope none of you will ever have such an experience of this depression of spirit as I have had; yet I have learnt from it to be very tender with all fellow-sufferers. The Lord have mercy on them and help them out of the Slough of Despond; for if He does not, they will sink in deep mire, where there is no standing."[343]

Coping with depression. Paul said, "I think you ought to know, dear brothers, about the hard time we went through in Asia. We were really crushed and overwhelmed, and feared we would never live through it" (2 Corinthians 1:8 TLB). Kent Hughes remarks, "With the resounding comfort of God still sounding (2 Corinthians 1:3–7), Paul now relates a dramatic personal example of God's care. His despair is framed in memorable terms because the Greek words translated 'For we were so utterly burdened beyond our strength' were also used to describe an overloaded ship riding low in the water so that it cannot rise. Paul was so 'utterly, unbearably crushed' (RSV) that he couldn't get up. Inertia gripped his being so much he 'despaired of life itself.' His despair was so deep that he was literally 'without a way of escape.' There was no exit." [344] How did he survive the ordeal? By exhibiting confidence in God by relying upon Him alone for rescue (2 Corinthians 1:9–10), the prayers of others (2 Corinthians 1:11), and dependence upon grace (2 Corinthians 1:12).

Spurgeon found relief from the torment of depression in several ways. He faced it honestly. He says, "I am heartily ashamed of myself for falling into [despondency], but I am sure there is no remedy for it like a holy faith in God."[345]

He sought to see God's hand or purpose in it. In the sermon "For the Troubled," Spurgeon said, "As long as I trace my pain to accident, my bereavement to mistake, my loss to another's wrong, my discomfort to an enemy, and so on, I am of the earth, earthy, and shall break my teeth with gravel stones; but when I rise to my God and see His hand at work, I grow calm. I have not a word of repining."[346] Writing in *The Sword and the Trowel*, he said, "When the gold knows why and wherefore it is in the fire…[it] will thank the Refiner for putting it into the crucible and will find a sweet satisfaction even in the flames."[347] Obviously, the reason for the furnace, *if there is one*, is not always knowable. But searching for it is always a good place to start.

He combated it with the Sword of the Spirit. "The worst forms of depression," Spurgeon said, "are cured when Holy Scripture is believed."[348] See Psalm 119:28.

He found remedy through the power "of the peace-speaking power of the blood of Jesus, and His infinite love in dying upon the cross to put away all my transgressions."[349] See Revelation 12:11. In the sermon "Medicine for The Distracted," he said, "If you know the law of mental storms you may reach peace, and that law may be summed up in one line: Steer to God right away; fly to Him, and you will find a peaceful shelter."[350] Saith Spurgeon, "I am the subject of depressions of spirit so fearful that I hope none of you ever get to such extremes of misery as I go to, but I always get back again by this: I know I trust Christ. I have no reliance but in Him, and if He falls, I shall fall with Him. But if He does not, I shall not. Because He lives, I shall live also, and I spring to my legs again and fight with my depressions of spirit and get the victory through it. And so may you do, and so you must, for there is no other way of escaping from it."[351]

He thwarted it by remembering his spiritual estate. In the sermon "The Christian's Heaviness and Rejoicing," Spurgeon said, "What shall there be in all the depressions of spirits that can possibly come upon me that shall make me break my harp, even though I should for a moment hang it upon the willows? Do I not expect that yet again my songs shall mount to Heaven; and even now through the thick darkness do not the sparks of my joy appear, when I remember that I have still upon me the blood of Jesus, and still about me the glorious righteousness of the Messiah?"[352]

He found help through retreats to places like Mentone (the French Riviera), working in his garden, and walks in the countryside. He said, "Let a man be naturally as blithe as a bird, he will hardly be able to bear up year after year against such a suicidal process; he will make his study a prison and his books the warders of a goal [jail], while nature lies outside his window calling him to health and beckoning him to joy. The ferns and the rabbits, the streams and the trout, the fir trees and the squirrels, the primroses and the violets, the farm yard, the new-mown hay, and the fragrant hops—these are the best medicine for hypochondriacs, the surest tonics for the declining, the best refreshments for the weary."[353]

And, for him, cigars were of "medicinal value" (he did not count it a sin), providing means of rest and relief. "I have felt grateful to God," he wrote to the *Daily Telegraph,* "when I have found intense pain relieved, a weary brain soothed, and calm, refreshing sleep obtained by a cigar."[354] Note: Spurgeon was known to smoke a cigar occasionally, one or perhaps two a day, making sure it never became an addiction. It is likely he smoked to the end of his life.[355]

> These infirmities may be no detriment to a man's career of special usefulness.
> Charles Spurgeon

Depression doesn't invalidate the call to ministry; it actually can be used by God to enhance it. Lecturing to students studying for the ministry at his college, Spurgeon said, "These infirmities may be no detriment to a man's career of special usefulness; they may even have been imposed upon him by divine wisdom as necessary qualifications for his peculiar course of service. Pain has probably in some cases developed genius."[356] Continuing, he said, "The ministries of Jeremiah are as acceptable as those of Isaiah, and even the sullen Jonah is a true prophet."[357]

In *Morning and Evening* Spurgeon said, "Let me lie, a poor broken shell, washed up by His love, having no virtue or value; but knowing that if He will bend His ear to me, He will hear within my heart faint echoes of the vast waves of His own love that have brought me to where I am happy to stay, even at His feet forever."[358]

In times of depression (per Spurgeon's example), cry out to God for deliverance, rely upon His promises to help, get rest, spend time outdoors walking, and don't hesitate to confide in friends and consult with doctors (sadly, doctors of his day, unlike now, were inapt to help much). Spurgeon, in the sermon "The Cause and Cure of a Wounded Spirit," speaks counsel to those who struggle with depression: "Do not, therefore, think that you are quite alone in your sorrow. Bow your head and bear it if it cannot be removed; for but a little while and every cloud shall be swept away, and you, in the cloudless sunlight, shall behold your God."[359]

In a lecture to the students at the Pastors' College, Spurgeon summarized how the minister is to cope with depression: "Cast the burden of the present, along with the sin of the past and the fear of the future, upon the Lord, who forsaketh not His saints. Live by the day—aye, by the hour. Put no trust in feelings. Trust in God alone and lean not on the reeds of human help. Be not surprised when friends fail you; it is a failing world. Continue with double earnestness to serve your Lord when no visible result is before you. In nothing let us be turned aside from the path which the divine call has urged us to pursue. Come fair or come foul, the pulpit is our watchtower and the ministry our warfare; be it ours, when we cannot see the face of our God, to trust UNDER THE SHADOW OF HIS WINGS."[360]

14

The Preacher's Conflict with a Barnabas

"Conflicts bring experience, and experience brings that growth in grace which is not to be attained by any other means."[361] ~ C. H. Spurgeon

Paul's sharp disagreement with Barnabas about John Mark ended their joint ministry (Acts 15:37–40). Barnabas wanted to take John Mark on the next missionary journey, but Paul didn't because Mark had deserted them in the heat of ministry in Pamphylia (Proverbs 25:19). John MacArthur comments, "This was not an amicable parting—they were in sharp disagreement regarding John Mark. The weight of the evidence favors Paul's decision, especially since he was an apostle of Jesus Christ. That alone should have caused Barnabas to submit to his authority."[362] Matthew Henry says, "It is a pity that they did not refer the matter to a third person, or that some friend did not interpose to prevent its coming to an open rupture."[363]

"A few hot words may undo the love of years, as a few blows of the axe cuts down the oak of a century's growth."[364] The deep and meaningful relationship of Paul and Barnabas shouldn't have ended so abruptly, but it sadly did due to their bitter argument. The conflict inflicted a heart wound that never completely healed. "As small a matter as it was, it waxed to a separation, and to disjoin these two in body as well as in mind."[365]

Matthew Henry insightfully states, "Paul and Barnabas, who were not separated by the persecutions of the unbelieving Jews, nor the impositions of the believing Jews, were yet separated by an unhappy disagreement between themselves. Oh, the mischief that even the poor and weak remainders of pride and passion that are found even in good men do in the world, do in the church! No wonder the consequences are so fatal where they reign."[366]

Disagreements that lead to separation among godly ministry leaders happen. Sometimes it is for the best. In the case of Barnabas and Paul, the division doubled the missionary force (Paul with Silas, and Barnabas with John Mark). The spiritual giants remained committed to their intention prior to the dispute, namely to 'visit their brethren in every city, where they had preached the Word of God' (Acts 15:36).

Give the men credit for not allowing Satan to use the conflict to stop the work of the ministry. Barnabas and Mark go to Cyprus (part of the territory where Mark had been faithful on the first tour), and Paul and his new associate, Silas, go to the part of the country that Mark did not visit earlier. Despite personnel disagreements and replacements, keep preaching. Keep singing. Keep teaching. Keep going and sowing. Keep doing the work of the ministry.

Scripture alludes to the reconciliation between Paul and Barnabas and John Mark. In Paul's letter to the Corinthians ten years following their dispute, he wrote kindly of Barnabas (1 Corinthians 9:6). With regard to John Mark, he tells Timothy to bring him to see him, for he is "profitable to me for the ministry" (2 Timothy 4:11). See Matthew 5:24.

> When two men cannot agree to toil in the same corner of the vineyard, let them honestly divide and betake them to other departments.
>
> Joseph Parker

However, he never reunited with Barnabas. "Sometimes you have to move on without certain people; if they're meant to be in your life, they will catch up."[367] Saith Joseph Parker, "When two men cannot agree to toil in the same corner of the vineyard, let them honestly divide and betake them to other departments."[368] But, like Paul and Barnabas, let them separate without "splitting the church" or creating chaos in the membership.

Fortunately, team leadership dispute was not an issue for Spurgeon. He was a solo pastor until 1868 when James Spurgeon, his brother, became co-pastor due to Spurgeon's ill health, and in 1891 when William Stott was appointed assistant-minister for the year[369]. But neither did he encounter conflict with his church officers (nine deacons[370] and twenty-five elders[371]) and congregation at large. He testified, "I have never been the pastor of a dead church, controlled by dead deacons.…All my church officers are in a very real sense my brethren in Christ."[372] Church business meeting minutes record no evidence of faction or fighting within the Metropolitan Tabernacle congregation or disagreement with the elders or deacons.[373]

15
The Preacher's Damaged Reputation

"If a man blows out the candle of a Christian's reputation, God will light it again. If He does not do so in this life, remember that at the resurrection there will be a resurrection of reputations as well as bodies: 'Then shall the righteous shine forth as the sun in the kingdom of their Father.'"[374] ~ C. H. Spurgeon

Paul was counted by Christian Jews as a troublemaker (Acts 21:21). He said, "Right now we have become garbage in the eyes of the world and trash in the sight of all people" (1 Corinthians 4:13b GW). How did he respond? "When our reputations are attacked, we remain courteous" (1 Corinthians 4:13a GW).

Of reputations soiled for Christ's sake, Spurgeon said, "I felt quite sure that if my reputation should be lost here among men it would be safe with my Lord; for at the day of judgment there will be a resurrection of reputations as well as of bodies."[375] Eggs from the chickens Charles and Susannah raised at their home were always sold, never given away, even to the closest of relatives. As a result, some counted them greedy, a criticism they accepted without defense. Both remained silent in defense because they didn't want the "right hand" to know what the "left hand" was doing (Matthew 6:3). Not until after their death was it learned that all the profits from the sale of eggs went to support two elderly widows.[376] Their reputation was vindicated.

But far more seriously and with greater ramifications his reputation was marred during the "Downgrade Controversy" (a courageous stand he took against doctrinal decay in the Baptist Union). Writing in "Lion in Winter" he asserted that his vindication would come in time. And it did, but long after his death. Jason Kallen wrote, "Indeed, Spurgeon has been vindicated. The British Baptist Union is a shadow of its former self. Moreover, Spurgeon's Downgrade foreshadowed the Fundamentalist/Modernist Controversy of the 1920s and the great SBC Controversy at the end of the 20th century. Doctrinal decay always brings dire consequences."[377] Every minister that takes a biblical and doctrinal stance as Spurgeon did may be presently maligned and have his reputation assaulted, but in time he will be exonerated.

About suffering injury of reputation Spurgeon said, "It was my lot to go through two or three years of the most violent abuse, and I thank God for it. I felt it very hard to bear, but I fell upon my knees before God and told Him that when I gave Him everything else, I gave Him my character too. If I had known that by faithfully serving Christ I must ruin my reputation, I think I should not have paused for a single moment."[378]

Every reputation that has been obscured by clouds of reproach for Christ's sake shall be rendered glorious when the righteous shall shine forth as the sun in the kingdom of their Father.

Charles Spurgeon

In the sermon "Assured Security in Christ," Spurgeon addresses the subject of a preacher's damaged reputation: "A Christian minister must expect to lose his repute among men. He must be willing to suffer every reproach for Christ's sake. But then he may rest assured that he will never lose his real honor if it be risked for the truth's sake and placed in the Redeemer's hand. The day shall declare the excellence of the upright, for it will reveal all that was hidden and bring to the light that which was concealed. There will be a resurrection of characters as well as persons. Every reputation that has been obscured by clouds of reproach for Christ's sake shall be rendered glorious when the righteous shall shine forth as the sun in the kingdom of their Father. Let the wicked say what they will of me, said the apostle, I commit my character to the Judge of quick and dead."[379]

16
The Preacher's Ministerial Fear

"We need indomitable, dogged resolution, and a combination of sacred obstinacy, self-denial, holy gentleness, and invincible courage."[380] ~ C. H. Spurgeon

Paul testifies that he knew what it was to be 'much afraid' (1 Corinthians 2:3). He was beaten and imprisoned in Philippi, driven out of Thessalonica and Berea, stoned and left for dead in Lystra, and scoffed at in Athens. But it was not for such things that Paul was afraid (2 Timothy 1:7). He feared letting Christ down.

John MacArthur states, "His fear and shaking were because of the seriousness of his mission."[381] Matthew Henry comments, "None know the fear and trembling of faithful ministers, who are zealous over souls with a godly jealousy; and a deep sense of their own weakness is the occasion of this fear and trembling. They know how insufficient they are, and are therefore fearful for themselves."[382] "Martin Luther, who never feared the face of man, yet declared that when he stood up to preach, he often felt his knees knock together under a sense of his great responsibility."[383]

Spurgeon was often overcome with sickening fear prior to preaching. In 1861 he remarked, "My deacons know well enough how, when I first preached in Exeter Hall, there was scarcely ever an occasion in which they left me alone for ten minutes before the service but they would find me in a most fearful state of sickness, produced by that tremendous thought of my solemn responsibility."[384] Later in ministry the nausea was thwarted, but not the anxiety.

In a sermon preached at Belfast, in August 1858, he said, "I can say, and God is my witness, that I never yet feared the face of man, be he who or what he may; but I often tremble— *yea, I always do*—in ascending the pulpit, lest I should not faithfully proclaim the Gospel to poor perishing sinners. The anxiety of rightly preparing and delivering a discourse so that the preacher may fully preach Christ to his hearers and pray them in Christ's stead to be reconciled to God is such as only he knows who loves the souls of men. It is no child's play to be the occupant of a pulpit; he who finds it to be so may find it to be something more fearful than Devil's play when the day of judgment shall come."[385]

And in 1883 he stated, "I have preached the Gospel now these thirty years and more, and…I tremble like an aspen leaf.

And often in coming down to this pulpit have I felt my knees knock together—not that I am afraid of any one of my hearers, but I am thinking of that account which I must render to God, whether I speak His Word faithfully or not."[386] In the sermon "Scourge for Slumbering Souls," he shared, "I have come here some Sunday mornings with the burden of the Lord upon my heart until I have been bowed down with the weight, and there is not a Sunday night, and has not been for many a day, when I do not come onto this platform in such a state both of body and soul that I pity a dog who has to suffer what I have, under the terror and the weight of the awful responsibility of having to preach to such a crowd as this."[387] In this he was like John Knox, who said, "I have never once feared the Devil, but I tremble every time I enter the pulpit."

Spurgeon may have feared failing God in his preaching, but he certainly wasn't afraid of man or personal harm. In his first year as pastor in London (1854) at New Park Street Chapel (later to become Metropolitan Tabernacle), the great cholera pandemic swept through the city killing ten thousand, among which were many of his church members. Instead of cowering, Spurgeon visited the sick and dying. He recounts efforts to help them in his autobiography. "During that epidemic of cholera, though I had many engagements in the country, I gave them up that I might remain in London to visit the sick and the dying. I felt that it was my duty to be on the spot in such a time of disease and death and sorrow. All day, and sometimes all night long, I went about from house to house and saw men and women dying, and, oh, how glad they were to see my face! When many were afraid to enter their houses lest they should catch the deadly disease, we who had no fear about such things found ourselves most gladly listened to when we spoke of Christ and of things divine."[388]

He acknowledged that the work caused him to be "weary in body and sick in heart" as he witnessed friends dying one by one, to the point he himself was about to faint. Upon returning from a funeral, he noticed a bulletin in a storefront window that bore the words: "Because thou hast made the LORD, which is my refuge, even the most High, thy habitation; there shall no evil befall thee, neither shall any plague come nigh thy dwelling" (Psalm 91:9–10). Of that "providential" experience he states, "The effect upon my heart was immediate. Faith appropriated the passage as her own. I felt secure, refreshed, girt with immortality. I went on with my visitation of the dying in a calm and peaceful spirit; I felt no fear of evil, and I suffered no harm."[389]

"Adversities may darken around us," comments G. T. Perks, "difficulties may menace us, men may frown, and devils rage; but with the eye of God upon us, with the life of God within us, and with the Heaven of God before us, we shall be able to breast the storm and to seize the crown."[390]

17
The Preacher's Wear-Out

"There may be here and there men of iron, to whom wear and tear work no perceptible detriment, but surely the rust frets even these; and as for ordinary men, the Lord knows, and makes them to know, that they are but dust."[391] ~ C. H. Spurgeon

Paul knew exhaustion in Christian service from the strenuous hard work and long days it entailed 'struggling, striving, or fighting' (Colossians 1:29a). He didn't punch the clock; he worked around the clock (2 Thessalonians 3:8b). Paul, although often in "weariness" ["exhaustive labor"], did not become "weak" (2 Corinthians 11:27, 29) or experience "burnout" because he served not in human strength but in the 'power' of the Holy Spirit (Colossians 1:29b).

Spurgeon was always working for the Savior. In his autobiography he says, "I could scarcely content myself even for five minutes without trying to do something for Christ."[392] And this brought on ministry fatigue. He once remarked, "No one living knows the toil and care I have to bear. I ask for no sympathy but ask for indulgence if I sometimes forget something. I have to look after the Orphanage, have charge of a church with four thousand members; sometimes there are marriages and burials to be undertaken; there is the weekly sermon to be revised, *The Sword and the Trowel* to be edited, and besides all that, a weekly average of five hundred letters to be answered."[393] (A detailed description of how the Sunday sermon manuscript was revised by Spurgeon each Monday morning for publication is set forth in C. H. Spurgeon's *Autobiography* (Vol. 2): *A Full Harvest,* 318–324. In addition, he chose to personally interview each new member candidate prior to initiating further consideration of their membership.[394] In the first six and a half years Spurgeon was pastor at New Park Chapel they received 1,442 new members—that meant 1,442 personal interviews with him. Spurgeon believed that not a seat in the Tabernacle was without its convert.[395]

I could scarcely content myself even for five minutes without trying to do something for Christ.

Charles Spurgeon

Saith Spurgeon, "Why are many earnest ministers worn and weary till heart and brain give way? They would be of little use if they did not run such a risk. All men who are eminently useful are made to feel their weakness in a supreme degree."[396] In 1872, in the sermon "Laboring and Not Fainting," Spurgeon stated, "The ministry is a matter which wears the brain and strains the heart and drains out the life of a man if he attends to it as he should."[397] While preaching on a Sunday when he exhausted, he stopped and sat down while the church sang a hymn. (Ever felt like doing that?) Afterward, with difficulty, he finished the sermon. Saith Spurgeon, "We can only produce life in others by the wear and tear of our own being."[398]

He continues, "If by excessive labor we die before reaching the average age of man, worn out in the Master's service, then glory be to God. We shall have so much less of earth and so much more of Heaven! It is our duty and privilege to exhaust our lives for Jesus." And this Spurgeon did, which no doubt attributed to his death on January 31, 1892, at age 57. Lord Shaftesbury said of Spurgeon, "The list of associations [he founded 66 ministries, planted more than 200 churches, wrote about 150 books, and every week preached four to ten times] instituted by his genius and superintended by his care were more than enough to occupy the minds and hearts of fifty ordinary men."[399] And with his assessment I more than heartedly agree after the hundreds of hours of research invested into the study of his life and ministry.

Did Spurgeon overtax himself? Were there times when he had too much on his plate? Some think so, but obviously he didn't. During his first serious illness Spurgeon wrote to his congregation from Clapham on October 26, 1858: "Do not attribute this illness to my having labored too hard for my Master. For His dear sake I would that I may yet be able to labor more."[400] Later, in the sermon "Gospel Missions," he stated, "I look with pity upon people who say 'Do not preach so often; you will kill yourself.' Oh, my God! What would Paul have said to such a thing as that?"[401]

In the sermon "For the Sick and Afflicted," preached in 1876, he addressed the matter of his health again. He said, "People said to me years ago, 'You will break your constitution down with preaching ten times a week,' and the like. Well, if I have done so, I am glad of it. I would do the same again. If I had fifty constitutions, I would rejoice to break them down in the service of the Lord Jesus Christ."[402] And then he gave a challenge: "Fight for the Lord while you can.

You will never regret having done all that lies in you for our blessed Lord and Master."[403] Lecturing to the students at the Pastors' College he frankly said, "In every minister's life there should be traces of stern labor."[404]

In the sermon "Suffering and Reigning with Jesus," he gives reason for the minister's "excessive" work (including his own): "We are all too much occupied with taking care of ourselves; we shun the difficulties of excessive labor. And frequently behind the entrenchments of taking care of our constitution, we do not half as much as we ought. A minister of God is bound to spurn the suggestions of ignoble ease. It is his calling to labor; and if he destroys his constitution, I, for one, only thank God that He permits us the high privilege of so making ourselves living sacrifices."[405] "We ought always to preach," asserts Spurgeon, "as though we should go out of the pulpit into Heaven, always to pray in that way, and always to spend every day as if we had not another day to spend. For this we need much of the Holy Spirit's power."[406]

Note, Spurgeon sought periods of rest and retreat from his labors. But that which kept him going was the inner rest of his soul that possessed him. In the sermon "Rest, Rest," he remarks, "True rest to the mind of the child of God is rest on the wing, rest in motion, rest in service, not rest with the yoke off, but with the yoke on. Every active Christian will tell you he is never happier than when he has much to do, and on the whole, if he communes with Jesus, never more at rest than when he has least leisure. Look not for your rest in the mere enjoyments and excitements of religion, but find your rest in wearing a yoke which you love, and which, for that reason, is easy to your neck."[407]

And then he says, "The rest of the Christian is found not in cowardice but in courage; it lies not in providing for ease but in the brave endurance of suffering for the truth. The restful spirit counts the reproach of Christ to be greater riches than all the treasures of Egypt; he falls in love with the cross and counts the burden light, and so finds rest in service and rest in suffering. Note that well."[408] Most ministers are in less danger of "burn-out" or "wear-out" than of "rust-out."

18
The Preacher's Abandonment

"My heart has been ready to sink within me....Friends have forsaken me."[409] ~ C. H. Spurgeon

Paul was deserted by the Christians of Rome when on trial. Of that time he said, "No man stood with me" (2 Timothy 4:16). But God did (2 Timothy 4:17). And Spurgeon likewise had his fair-weather friends and deserters. In a letter to James Watts Borough dated Tuesday, April 1855, Spurgeon wrote: "Scarcely a Baptist minister of standing will own me! I am sick of man; but when I find a good one, I love him all the better because of the contrast to others."[410] In 1888, Spurgeon was forsaken by friends and alumni of the Pastors' College (numbering eighty) when he withdrew from the Baptist Union.[411] Of that abandonment, Spurgeon wrote in a letter to a friend, "I cannot tell you by letter what I have endured in the desertion of my own men."[412]

Friendship has been the cause of the greatest misery to men when it has been unworthy and unfaithful.

Charles Spurgeon

Being forsaken by "friends" is to be anticipated. Spurgeon says, "Be not surprised when friends fail you. The disciples of Jesus forsook Him; be not amazed if your adherents wander away to other teachers."[413] Tearfully, no doubt, he further said, "Counterfeits of friendships are common as autumn leaves,"[414] and, "The world's friendship is ever brittle."[415]

"Friendship," saith Spurgeon, "has been the cause of the greatest misery to men when it has been unworthy and unfaithful."[416] Giving cautionary counsel to the students at the Pastors' College, he said, "Trust in God and lean not on the needs of human help. Be not surprised when friends fail you. Never count upon immutability in man; inconstancy you may reckon upon with fear of disappointment."[417]

The preacher needs real friends that stick by him through thick and thin. Spurgeon is correct: "Many might have failed beneath the bitterness of their trial had they not found a friend."[418]

What kind of friend(s) ought the preacher to embrace? Spurgeon says the kind that "having once given his heart to his chosen companion, he clings to him in all weathers, fair or foul; he loves him none the less because he becometh poor or because his fame suffers an eclipse, but his friendship like a lamp shines the brighter, or is made more manifest because of the darkness that surrounds it. True friendship is not fed from the barn floor or the wine fat; it is not like the rainbow dependent upon the sunshine. It is fixed as a rock and firm as granite and smiles superior to wind and tempest."[419] To Spurgeon, one such friend was William Harrald.

"Be friendly to all, but make none your friends until they know you and you know them."[420] Take the time to build genuine and permanent friendships. Saith Spurgeon, "True friendship must not be of hasty growth. As quaint old Master Fuller says, 'Let friendship creep gently to a height; if it rushes to it, it may soon run itself out of breath.'"[421] "If you receive the heart of a friend," Spurgeon said, "mind you give him back your own."[422]

A sketch shows Winnie the Pooh and Piglet walking hand in hand down the road with the caption, "Never forget who was there for you when no one else was." When others rush for the exit, a true friend abides, like William Harrald. Preacher, "make sure thy friend" (Prov. 6:3).

19

The Preacher's Death Threats

"We feel we are immortal till our work is done; we feel that God is with us, and that we are bound to be victorious through the blood of Jesus. We shall not be defeated in the campaign of life, for the Lord of hosts is with us, and we shall tread down our enemies."[423] ~ C. H. Spurgeon

Paul's life was threatened in Lystra where he was stoned and left for dead (Acts 14:19). It was threatened at the Temple where the crowd cried out, "Away with such a fellow from the earth: for it is not fit that he should live" (Acts 22:22). When he was jailed in Jerusalem, it was threatened again by a conspiracy of more than forty men who pledged not to eat or drink until they had killed him (Acts 23:12–16). There were at least four attempts on Spurgeon's life (almost stabbed with a knife, bludgeoned with a stick, hung from the neck, and blown up by a bomb[424]).

If, like Paul and Spurgeon, your life is threatened, hunker down at the foot of the Cross in dependence upon God who is your able refuge, defender, and strong tower. The Scripture gives promise: "He will spread his wings over you and keep you secure. His faithfulness is like a shield or a city wall. You won't need to worry about dangers at night or arrows during the day" (Psalm 91:4–5 CEV). See Matthew 10:28.

Coupled with prayer, God would have you act prudently. When he learned of the plot against his life in Jerusalem by forty men, Paul urged that the chief captain of the prison be informed (Acts 23:16–24). That move saved his life and ministry.

If the preacher can avoid death without compromising the faith and loyalty to Christ, then upon the leadership of the Holy Spirit it ought to be done. There is biblical precedent for the response. God instructed Elijah to avoid death by King Ahab by hiding (1 Kings 19:1–18). God told Joseph to flee to Egypt with the Christ-child to avoid the baby's death (Matthew 2:13–18). Jesus told the disciples that if they are persecuted in one city, "flee ye into another" (Matthew 10:23). "The flight was not, therefore, a flight from suffering [and death], but a flight in order to fulfill the mission of Christ. While God's word can go out forcefully through the testimony of martyrdom, it is sometimes better that people remain alive in order to proclaim it (Acts 14:5–6)."[425]

In Spurgeon's sermon "My Times Are in Thy Hand," he voices encouragement for the minister facing death threats for Christ's sake: "The close of life is not decided by the sharp knife of the fates, but by the hand of love. We shall not die before our time; neither shall we be forgotten and left upon the stage too long....My times are in those hands which were nailed to the cross for my redemption (Psalm 31:15)."[426]

> Plagues and deaths around me fly;
> Till He bids, I cannot die.
> Not a single shaft can hit,
> Till the God of love sees fit. ~ John Ryland (1777)

In the next to final sermon Spurgeon revised (all were noticeably edited prior to printing), he said, "O worker for God, death cannot touch thy sacred mission! Be thou content to die if the truth shall live the better because thou diest. When the sepulcher receives this mortal frame, we shall not die, but live."[427]

20

The Preacher's Crushing Hardship

"Be of good courage. There are few storms, after all, that are ahead, to those that have passed through many already. The further we are on the road, the less there is of it to bear."[428] ~ C. H. Spurgeon

To Paul and Spurgeon hardship was such a norm of ministry (par for the course) that the former told Timothy, "Join with me in suffering, like a good soldier of Christ Jesus" (2 Timothy 2:3 NIV), and the latter declared, "When we are in a battle, we must expect calamities."[429] Rose-colored glasses about ministry lead to disillusionment, discouragement and despair.

Note Paul's readiness to suffer. He says, "I am ready not to be bound only, but also to die at Jerusalem for the name of the Lord Jesus" (Acts 21:13). Saith Spurgeon: "To be ready to suffer is more than to be ready to serve. To some of us it has become a habit to be ready to preach the Gospel; but here was a man who was ready to suffer for the name of the Lord Jesus, so ready that he could not be dissuaded from it. He might preach the Gospel, but why must he go to Jerusalem? All the world was before him; why must he go to that persecuting city? Everybody told him that he would have bonds and imprisonment and perhaps death,; but he cared nothing about all that. He said, 'I am ready, I am ready.'"[430]

A Christian man is seldom long at ease;
When one trouble's gone, another does him seize.[431]

Saith Spurgeon, "Men will never become great in divinity until they become great in suffering. 'Ah!' said Luther, 'affliction is the best book in my library'; and let me add, the best leaf in the book of affliction is that blackest of all the leaves, the leaf called heaviness, when the spirit sinks within us and we cannot endure as we could wish. And yet again, this heaviness is of essential use to a Christian if he would do good to others. There are none so tender as those who have been skinned themselves. Those who have been in the chamber of affliction know how to comfort those who are there. Do not believe that any man will become a physician unless he walks the hospitals, and I am sure that no one will become a divine or become a comforter unless he lies in the hospital as well as walks through it, and has to suffer himself."[432]

In the sermon "Cheering Words and Solemn Warnings," Spurgeon says, "The Christian gains by his losses. He acquires health by his sickness. He wins friends through his bereavements, and he becomes a conqueror through his defeats. Nothing, therefore, can be injurious to the Christian, when the very worst things that he has are but rough waves to wash his golden ships home to port and enrich him."[433]

> Even if the enemy's foot be on your neck,
> expect to rise and overthrow him.
> Charles Spurgeon

"Wait a little longer. Ah, beloved!" Spurgeon exhorts, "how despicable our troubles and trials will seem when we look back upon them! Looking at them here in the prospect, they seem immense; but when we get to Heaven, they will seem to us just nothing at all. Let us go on, therefore; and if the night be ever so dark, remember there is not a night that shall not have a morning, and that morning is to come by-and-by."[434] Saith Spurgeon, "Even if the enemy's foot be on your neck, expect to rise and overthrow him."[435]

21
The Preacher's Pride

"He who thinks that he is somebody is nobody—and he whose head swims because of his elevation will soon have it broken because of his tumbling down from his lofty position."[436] ~ C. H. Spurgeon

Matthew Henry asserts, "The greater the gifts are, the more the possessor is exposed to temptations, and the larger is the measure of grace needed to keep him humble and spiritual."[437]

John Stott writes, "Pride is without doubt the chief occupational hazard of the preacher. It has ruined many and deprived their ministry of power....In some it is blatantly obvious. They are exhibitionists by temperament and use the pulpit as a stage on which they show off....Other preachers are not like Nebuchadnezzars, however, for their pride does not take the form of blatant boastfulness. It is more subtle, more insidious, and even more perverse. For it is possible to adopt an outward demeanor of great meekness, while inside our appetite for applause is insatiable."[438]

Spurgeon remarked, "We must put away all notion of self-importance. God will not bless the man who thinks himself great. To glory even in the work of God the Holy Spirit in yourself is to tread dangerously near to self-adulation. 'Let another...praise thee,...and not thine own lips,' and be very glad when that other has sense enough to hold his tongue."[439] "Say much of what the Savior has done for you, but say little of what you have done for the Lord. Do not utter a self-glorifying sentence."[440]

In the sermon "Pride and Humility," Spurgeon warns of pride's deceptiveness: "Oh! my friends, you cannot tell how *many shapes pride will assume*; look sharp about you, or you will be deceived by it, and when you think you are entertaining angels, you will find you have been receiving devils unawares."[441]

The preacher who reeks with a spirit of haughtiness, conceit, and pride not only impedes his ministry but that of the church. See Titus 1:7. Adrian Rogers states, "Pride is such a deceitful sin. Many people who are infected and infested with pride have no idea that they are. As a matter of fact, the proud person is often very proud of his humility."[442]

Saith Spurgeon, "And pride will grow in the pulpit. It is a weed that is dreadfully rampant. It wants cutting down every week, or else we should stand up to our knees in it. This pulpit is a shocking bad soil for pride. It grows terribly, and I scarcely know whether you ever find a preacher of the Gospel who will not confess that he has the greatest temptation to pride. Many men have been held up by the arms of men; they have been held up by the arms of praise, and not of prayer. These arms have become weak, and down they have fallen. I say there is temptation to pride in the pulpit, but there is no ground for it in the pulpit."[443]

In *Morning and Evening* he states, "When God's warrior marches forth to battle strong in his own might, when he boasts, 'I know that I shall conquer; my own right arm and my conquering sword shall get unto me the victory,' defeat is not far distant. God will not go forth with that man who marches in his own strength. He who reckoneth on victory thus has reckoned wrongly, for 'it is not by might, nor by power, but by my Spirit, saith the Lord of hosts.'"[444]

Adversity, especially the "thorn in the flesh," Paul attests, prevented an attitude of arrogance and pride from developing in his heart. (If ever a man had grounds for boasting and pride in ministry about his abilities, giftedness, accomplishments, and trials, it was Paul [2 Corinthians 11:21–33]. But he refused. Rather, he said, "If I must boast, I will boast of the things that show my weakness" [2 Corinthians 10:30 NIV]).

Paul testifies, "I will say this: because these experiences I had were so tremendous, God was afraid I might be puffed up by them; so I was given a physical condition which has been a thorn in my flesh, a messenger from Satan to hurt and bother me and prick my pride" (2 Corinthians 12:7 TLB). The thorn that plagued him was a divine means of humbling him that God might use him mightily. Saith Spurgeon, "Those who are honored of their Lord in public have usually to endure a secret chastening, or to carry a peculiar cross, lest by any means they exalt themselves, and fall into the snare of the devil."[445]

Pride is yet my darling sin; I cannot shake it off.
Charles Spurgeon

Spurgeon's secret sin was pride, a sin which he deeply abhorred. (Consider the temptation for him to be boastful and egotistical—the most popular preacher in the world at age 22, pastor of the largest protestant church in the world, kings and queens sought his audience, considered the "Prince of Preachers," etc.). He recorded in his diary: "Pride is yet my darling sin; I cannot shake it off."[446] In a letter to a friend, he confessed, "My pride is so infernal that there is not a man on earth who can hold it in."[447] He said, "Oh, may I be kept humble! Pride dwells in my heart."[448]

In the sermon "The Fifth Beatitude" he said: "For my own part, my constant prayer is that I may know the worst of my case, whatever the knowledge may cost me. I know that an accurate estimate of my own heart can never be otherwise than lowering to my self-esteem, but God forbid that I should be spared the humiliation which springs from the truth! The sweet red apples of self-esteem are deadly poison; who would wish to be destroyed thereby? The bitter fruits of self-knowledge are always healthful, especially if washed down with the waters of repentance and sweetened with a draught from the wells of salvation; he who loves his own soul will not despise them."[449]

In *Morning and Evening* he warns, "If we forget to live at the foot of the cross in deepest lowliness of spirit, God will not forget to make us smart under His rod."[450] The furnace of affliction was a means to Spurgeon's victory over pride, as it was with Paul. He said, "That is the benefit of the furnace to God's people: it melts, tries, and purifies them."[451]

George Whitefield also battled pride. One classic story reveals his temptation with it. "Mr. Whitefield, having delivered a discourse of rare beauty and eloquence in the city of Charleston, had just retired from the pulpit and was wending his way out of the church when he met an acquaintance in the aisle who, shaking him cordially by the hand, congratulated him on the splendid effort he had just made, saying, 'Brother Whitefield, you have preached a most eloquent discourse. I was highly delighted.' Whitefield, instead of being in the least elated, replied in the most solemn and impressive manner, 'Ah, brother, there is one in advance of you, for the Devil told me so before I left the pulpit.'"[452]

Horatius Bonar depicts the biblical preacher in saying, "He will be a humble man. He will think little and speak little about himself. True faith carries us above this pride, self-esteem, and vainglory....He will...refrain from giving prominence to self in any of his proceedings. His great object will be to hide self, and not only to forget it himself, but to make others forget it too. The man that is still proud, boastful, vainglorious, self-confident, has good reason to suppose that he has never yet believed."[453]

Spurgeon gives advice for the preacher struggling with pride: "Let us measure ourselves by our Master....then pride will be impossible."[454] He told his students, "The way to be very great is to be very little."[455] In the sermon "None but

Jesus," he exhorts, "Leave off boasting, Christian; live humbly before thy God, and never let a word of self-congratulation escape thy lips."[456] Further, he counsels, "Do not desire to be the principal man in the church. Be lowly. Be humble. The best man in the church is the man who is willing to be a doormat for all to wipe their boots on, the brother who does not mind what happens to him at all, so long as God is glorified."[457]

John Stott profoundly stated, "Nothing in history or in the universe cuts us down to size like the cross. All of us have inflated views of ourselves, especially in self-righteousness, until we have visited a place called Calvary. It is there, at the foot of the cross, that we shrink to our true size."[458]

And assuredly pray for power to thwart arrogance. Saith Spurgeon, "If you do not ascribe it to God, the temptation will be too strong for you; you will be sure to take it for yourself, and if you do this, the most fatal consequences will follow, for they that walk in pride, God will assuredly abase. No matter how dear you are to Him, if pride be harbored in your spirit, He will whip it out of you. They that go up in their own estimation must come down again by His discipline. You cannot be exalted in self without being by-and-by brought low before Him. God will have it so; it is always the rule: 'He hath put down the mighty from their seat, and hath exalted them of low degree.'"[459]

Solomon is right: "Pride goeth before destruction, and an haughty spirit before a fall" (Proverbs 16:18). J. I. Packer comments, "If we are not constantly growing downward into humility, we shall be steadily swelling up and running to seed under the influence of pride."[460]

Spurgeon, like Paul, progressed in humility to the degree that his son gave a note of it in remarks shared after his death. Charles Spurgeon, Jr., said, "There was one trait in his noble and godly character which, among many others, always shone with a luster peculiarly its own. His humility was of a Christlike character. Words of a eulogy concerning himself were ever painful to him; his motto in this, as in all other matters, being, 'Not I, but Christ.'"[461]

Spurgeon said, "Let my name perish, but let Christ's name last forever! I shall be quite content for you to go away and forget me."[462] He requested his interment be in Norwood cemetery, an inconspicuous place compared to what might have been chosen, among his church officers and many hundreds of church members.[463] In the lecture "What the Stones Say," Spurgeon asserts his view of tombstone epitaphs: "If anyone puts a gravestone over us, the less said about us, the better: our name, our birth, our death, and a godly text; but no fulsome flattery. Some gravestones have very much flattery on them, and the sooner the epitaphs are illegible, the better."[464]

In light of that view, it is no surprise that shortly before he died he whispered to William Harrald, "Remember, a plain stone. C. H. S. and No More; no fuss."[465] Such were the wishes for his tombstone, but slightly altered at the request of the deacons at the Metropolitan Tabernacle. Thomas Spurgeon (son) said, "It is satisfactory to know that if this wish has not been carried out in strict accord with its letter, its spirit has certainly been respected. At Norwood stands a substantial sepulcher with appropriate Scripture passages and emblems. But there is no fulsome flattery, and, thanks be to God, there is no possibility of tomb, or *Life,* or memory of him to be marred with any such 'Biographical Buts' as he referred to at the end of the lecture ["What the Stones Say"]. We glorify God in him."[466]

Even in the introduction to his autobiography, the mighty warrior exhibits humility, stating, "I think that the most interesting biography to any man is his own life....It would have been impossible for me to quote the experiences of other men if they had not been bold enough to record them, and I make an honest attempt to acknowledge my debt to my greater predecessors by writing down my own. Whether this arises from egotism or not each reader shall decide according to the sweetness or acidity of his own disposition. A father is excused when he tells his sons his own life story and finds it the readiest way to enforce his maxims; the old soldier is forgiven when he 'shoulders his crutch, and shows how fields were won'; I beg that the license which tolerates these may, on this occasion, be extended to me."[467]

Steeped in deep humility, Spurgeon, just four weeks before going to Heaven, confessed, "I look back and remember what I might have done and have not done, what opportunities of usefulness I have not seized, what sins I have allowed to pass unrebuked, what struggling beginners in grace I have failed to help. I cannot but grieve that what I have done was not done better or attended with a humbler dependence upon God."[468]

'Tis low, 'tis low,
Low down at His feet we bow;
'Tis low, 'tis low,
'Tis low at His feet we bow. ~ D. S. Warner (1911)

Saith Spurgeon, "Pride is as safely the sign of destruction as the change of mercury in the weather glass is the sign of rain. When men have ridden the high horse, destruction has always overtaken them."[469] William Law said, "You can have no greater sign of confirmed pride than when you think you are humble enough." D. L. Moody said, "A man can counterfeit love, he can counterfeit faith, he can counterfeit hope and all the other graces, but it is very difficult to counterfeit humility."[470] It is noteworthy that Spurgeon said of Moody in 1884 that he is "as devoid of self-importance as a new-born babe."[471] This humility was a key to Moody's great success. The way up is down. "He must increase, but I must decrease" (John 3:30).

> When a man is sincerely humble and never ventures to touch so much as a grain of the praise, there is scarcely any limit to what God will do for him.
> Charles Spurgeon

States Spurgeon, "You will never glory in God till first of all God has killed your glorying in yourself."[472] To this he adds in *Morning and Evening,* "When a man is sincerely humble and never ventures to touch so much as a grain of the praise, there is scarcely any limit to what God will do for him. Humility makes us ready to be blessed by the God of all grace and fits us to deal efficiently with our fellowmen. True humility is a flower which will adorn any garden. This is a sauce with which you may season every dish of life, and you will find an improvement in every case. Whether it be prayer or praise, whether it be work or suffering, the genuine salt of humility cannot be used in excess."[473]

22
The Preacher's Need

"The Lord will give enough, enough for all time, enough of all, enough for all, and more than enough. There shall be no real need of any believer but what the Lord will fill it full, and exceed it." [474] ~ C. H. Spurgeon

Paul's itinerant ministry, he states, was sustained by God ("tentmaking" and the saints). Writing to the Philippian saints he testifies, "And this same God who takes care of me will supply all your needs from his glorious riches, which have been given to us in Christ Jesus" (Philippians 4:19 NLT). He was content with the provision that God chose to give (Philippians 4:11–12) and honestly could say, "I have coveted no man's silver, or gold, or apparel" (Acts 20:33). Paul experienced firsthand that which David exclaimed, "The young lions do lack, and suffer hunger: but they that seek the LORD shall not want any good thing" (Psalm 34:10).

Saith Spurgeon, "Paul's God is our God and will supply all our need. Paul felt sure of this in reference to the Philippians, and we feel sure of it as to ourselves. God will do it, for it is like Him: He loves us, He delights to bless us, and it will glorify Him to do so. His pity, His power, His love, His faithfulness, all work together that we be not famished. What a measure doth the LORD go by: 'According to his riches in glory by Christ Jesus.' The riches of His grace are large, but what shall we say of the riches of His glory? His 'riches of glory by Christ Jesus'—who shall form an estimate of this? According to this immeasurable measure will God fill up the immense abyss of our necessities. He makes the LORD Jesus the receptacle and the channel of His fullness, and then He imparts to us His wealth of love in its highest form. Hallelujah!"[475]

To emphasize the heart of God to supply the "preacher's" need, Paul asks a rhetorical question: "He that spared not His own Son, but delivered Him up for us all, how shall He not with Him also freely give us all things?" (Romans 8:32).

Spurgeon, riding in an open carriage with William Hatcher near the entrance to the Stockwell Orphanage, pointed and said, "Yonder is my bank, where I get my money for taking care of my family of 500 children." Hatcher peered out the window but saw no bank. "There it is," said Spurgeon, pointing to a plaque cut into the wall which read: "Jehovah Jireh" (the Lord will provide). "That is my bank," said Spurgeon. "It never breaks, never suspends, never gets empty. My children have never lacked for covering, or for food, and I have no fear that they ever will."[476]

In the introduction to *Lectures to My Students,* Spurgeon said, "Our confidence is that God will supply all our means, and He has always done so hitherto."[477] To this he personally attested. "My witness is, and I speak it for the honor of God, that He is a good Provider. I have been cast upon the Providence of God ever since I left my father's house, and in all cases, He has been my Shepherd, and I have known no lack. My first income as a Christian minister was small enough in all conscience, never exceeding forty-five pounds a year; yet I was as rich then as I am now, for I had enough; and I had no more cares, nay, not half as many then as I have now; and when I breathed my prayer to God then, as I do now, for all things temporal and spiritual, I found Him ready to answer me at every pinch,—and full many pinches I have had."[478]

In the sermon "Filling the Empty Vessels," he states, "I have watched the ebb of the funds till nearly everything has been gone, and then I have joyfully said to myself, *Now for it! The vessels are empty. Now I shall see the miracle of filling them.* What wonders the Lord has worked for me, I cannot now tell you in detail, but many of you who have been my faithful helpers know how hundreds and even thousands of pounds have poured in from our great Lord in the moment of necessity. It will always be the same, for the Lord God is the same. Until the funds run low, we cannot expect to see them replenished. But when they get low, then will God come and deal graciously with us. Money is, however, our smallest need; we need grace, wisdom, light, and comfort, and these we shall have. All our needs are occasions for blessing. The more needs you have the more blessing you will get. God has promised to fill up all your needs. That is, all your empty vessels will be filled, and therefore, the more the merrier. Your extremity shall be an opportunity that God will use to show the riches of His grace."[479]

Hudson Taylor, a contemporary and friend of Spurgeon, provides encouragement: "Oh! beloved friends, if there is a living God, faithful and true, let us hold His faithfulness. Holding His faithfulness, we may go into every province of

China. Holding His faithfulness, we may face, with calm and sober but confident assurance of victory, every difficulty and danger. We may count on grace for the work, on pecuniary aid, on needful facilities, and on ultimate success. Let us not give Him a partial trust, but daily, hourly serve Him, 'holding God's faithfulness.'"[480] And "Depend on it! God's work done in God's way will never lack God's supply."[481]

> Despond then no longer; the Lord will provide,
> And this be the token
> No word He hath spoken
> Was ever yet broken; "the Lord will provide."
>
> March on, then, right boldly; the sea shall divide.
> The path shall be glorious,
> With shoutings victorious
> We'll join in the chorus: "The Lord will provide."
> ~ Martha A. W. Cook (1864)

Spurgeon illustrates how God provides the preacher's every need in the sermon "My Times Are in Thy Hand." He says, "Queen Elizabeth wished one of the leading merchants of London to go to Holland to watch her interests there. The honest man told her Majesty that he would obey her commands, but he begged her to remember that it would involve the ruin of his own trade for him to be absent. To this the Queen replied, "If you will see to my business, I will see to your business." With such a royal promise he might willingly let his own business go, for a queen should have it in her power to do more for a subject than he can do for himself. The Lord, in effect, says to the believer, 'I will take your affairs in hand and see them through for you.' Will you not at once feel that now it is your joy, your delight, to live to glorify your gracious Lord? To be set free to serve the Lord is the highest freedom."[482]

> As for His failing you, never dream of it—hate the
> thought of it. The God who has been sufficient
> until now should be trusted to the end.
>
> Charles Spurgeon

As you see to God's business, He most certainly will care for yours. This I bear witness to having served God fifty years as a vocational evangelist dependent wholly upon Him to supply my needs. Where God guides, He provides. Saith Spurgeon, "As for His failing you, never dream of it—hate the thought of it. The God who has been sufficient until now should be trusted to the end."[483]

Addressing the students at the Pastors' College, Spurgeon counseled, "Faith in God should tone down our concern about temporalities and enable us to practice what we preach; namely, 'Take no thought, saying, what shall we eat? or, what shall we drink; or, Wherewithal shall we be clothed? for your heavenly Father knoweth that ye have need of all these things'[484] (Matthew 6:31–32).

Note, "Spurgeon was never afraid to appeal for money, direct deacons of churches to cover students' expenses, or ask for a preaching fee which would be donated to the college."[485] But above all he trusted God to provide that which was needed in response to prayer.

23
The Preacher's Wounded Spirit

"Some have a wounded spirit through the cruelty of men, the unkindness of children, the ingratitude of those whom they have helped and for whom they have had such affection that they would almost have been willing to sacrifice their own lives."[486] ~ C. H. Spurgeon

Solomon says, "The spirit of a man will sustain his infirmity; but a wounded spirit who can bear?" (Proverbs 18:14). No minister is exempt from suffering a wounded spirit. If a mighty warrior as Spurgeon did, you and I certainly may. Spirit wounding may be defined as a crushing and bruising injury to the soul.

Saith Timothy Keller, "A crushed spirit is to look out at life and to have no desire for it, have little or no joy in it, have no passion to get out there and deal with it….There are degrees of a crushed spirit. It can be anywhere from listlessness and restlessness to discouragement to despondency to being very, very cast down and to losing all desire to live."[487] When the heart is sorely wounded, how doth the man of God yet preach and minister?

In the sermon "The Cause and Cure of a Wounded Spirit" Spurgeon relates how he suffered a wounded spirit thirty years earlier and thwarted it. He remarked, "It is a terrible wounding when he who should have been your friend becomes your foe, and when, like your Lord, you also have your Judas Iscariot. It is not easy to bear misrepresentation and falsehood, to have your purest motives misjudged, and to be thought to be only seeking something for yourself when you have a pure desire for the good of others. This is a very painful kind of wounded spirit."[488]

He continues by saying, "If thou wouldst bear thy trouble without complaining, if thou wouldst sustain thy burden without fainting, if though wouldst mount on wings as eagles, if thou wouldst run without weariness and walk without fainting, thou must have the life of God within thee; thou must be born again; thou must be in living union with Him who is the Strong One, and who, by the life which He implants within thee can give thee of His own strength….The kind of spirit, then, that a man needs to sustain his infirmity is one which has been renewed by the Holy Ghost and washed in the precious blood of Jesus….Bow your head and bear it, if it cannot be removed; for but a little while and every cloud shall be swept away, and you, in the cloudless sunlight, shall behold your God. Meanwhile, His strength is sufficient for you. He will not suffer you to be tempted above what you are able to bear; and if you cannot bear your infirmity because of your wounded spirit, He will bear for you both yourself and your infirmity. 'O rest in the Lord, and wait patiently for him.'"[489]

Then he states in the sermon "Healing for the Wounded," "Men may alleviate suffering; they may console the afflicted and cheer the distressed, but they cannot heal the broken in heart nor bind up their wounds. It is not human eloquence or mortal wisdom; it is not the oration of an Apollos nor the wondrous words of a prince of preachers; it is the 'still small voice' of God which alone confers the 'peace which passeth all understanding.'"[490]

Further, he counsels the wounded in spirit, "Remember Christ's *sympathy* with you. O thou who art tossed with tempest and not comforted, thy Lord's vessel is in the storm with thee! Yea, he is in the vessel with thee. There is not a pang that rends the believer's heart but he has felt it first. He drinks out of the cup with you. Is it very bitter? He has had a cup full of it for every drop that you taste. This ought to comfort you. I know of no better remedy for the heart's trouble in a Christian than to feel, 'My Master Himself takes no better portion than that which He gives to me.'"[491]

> Pressed beyond measure, yes, pressed to great length;
> Pressed so intensely, beyond my own strength;
> Pressed in my body and pressed in my soul;
> Pressed in my mind till the dark surges roll;
> Pressure from foes and pressure from dear friends;
> Pressure on pressure, till life nearly ends.

Pressed into knowing no helper but God;
Pressed into loving His staff and His rod;
Pressed into liberty where nothing clings;
Pressed into faith for impossible things;
Pressed into living my life for the Lord;
Pressed into living a Christ-life outpoured.
> ~ Annie Johnson Flint (1866–1932)

As one that has endured a wounded spirit at the hands of "friends," I know well its hurt and eventual healing. Therefore, with Spurgeon, I can say, "Do not despair, dear heart, but come to the Lord with all thy jagged wounds, black bruises, and running sores. He alone can heal, and He delights to do it. It is our Lord's office to bind up the brokenhearted, and He is gloriously at home at it."[492] "He healeth the broken in heart, and bindeth up their wounds" (Psalm 147:3).

24

The Preacher's Discouragement

"One crushing stroke has sometimes laid the minister very low."[493] ~ C. H. Spurgeon

Neither Paul nor Spurgeon were bulletproof from the dart of dark discouragement. Paul told the Christians at Corinth that in the work in Asia, he became pressed out of measure above his strength, that he became weary even of life (2 Corinthians 1:8). And Spurgeon confessed to his people that his worst enemy was the depths of despair and discouragement that he experienced for weeks or months at a time.

Of ministerial discouragement, he says, "I marvel not that the minister weeps—the wonder is he does not lament far more than he does!"[494] He explains, "Who can bear the weight of souls without sometimes sinking to the dust? Passionate longings after men's conversion, if not fully satisfied (and when are they?), consume the soul with anxiety and disappointment.

To see the hopeful turn aside, the godly grow cold, professors abusing their privileges, and sinners waxing more bold in sin—are not these sights enough to crush us to the earth? The kingdom comes not as we would, the reverend name is not hallowed as we desire, and for this we must weep."[495]

Spurgeon further describes the reason for pastoral discouragement: "When troubles multiply and discouragements follow each other in long succession like Job's messengers, then too amid the perturbation of soul occasioned by evil tidings, despondency despoils the heart of all its peace. If a scanty cupboard is rendered a severer trial by the sickness of a wife or the loss of a child, and if ungenerous remarks of hearers are followed by the opposition of deacons and the coolness of members, then, like Jacob, we are apt to cry, 'All these things are against me'. Accumulated distresses increase each other's weight. Wave upon wave is severe work for the strongest swimmer. The last ounce breaks the camel's back....what wonder if we for a while are ready to give up the ghost!"[496]

Discouragement looms with church conflict. Saith Spurgeon, "The fire of conflict is a terrible evil when it breaks out in a Christian church. Where there are converts and God is glorified, you will discover jealousy and envy doing the Devil's work most effectively."[497] Alfred Poirier says, "Christ is the reason many enter the pastorate. Conflict is the reason many leave."[498]

Discouragement looms with ministerial fruitlessness. Let the discouraged pastor be lifted by what Spurgeon states in the sermon "Cheer up, My Comrades!": "You may reasonably be sorrowful, but you have no right to despair. Non-success is a trial of faith which has been endured by many a trusty servant who has been triumphant in the issue. Did not the disciples toil all night and catch nothing? Did not our Lord say that some seed would fall on stony ground and some among the thorns, and that from these there would be no harvest? Do not, then, grudge the time or the strength you lay out in the service of our great Lord because you do not see your efforts thrive, for better men than you have wept over failure. Remember, too, that if you really do serve the Lord thoroughly and heartily, He will accept you and acknowledge your service, even though no good should come of it. It is your business to cast the bread on the waters; if you do not find it after many days, that is not your business. It is your business to scatter the seed."[499]

Expanding the consolation, he shared in the sermon "The King's Weighings," "If a man gives his life to convert the heathen and he does not succeed, he shall have as much reward of God as he who turns a nation to the faith. Two ministers have labored in the same field; the first preached the Gospel faithfully but saw scant results; the second, following him, found the rough work done and reaped full sheaves from the field. The thoughtless are apt to think the second man greatly superior to the first, but it is not so; one soweth and another reapeth. When God comes to weigh the actions of men, he may give greater praise to the sower than to the reaper."[500]

The Bible says, "The Lord is a God of knowledge, and by him actions are weighed" (1 Samuel 2:3). It is God that weighs the minister, not the congregation, public opinion, or ministerial association—and that He does compassionately and understandably.

A major cause for discouragement is bearing responsibilities that are not the pastor's to carry. Spurgeon asserts, "I hope you will always feel your responsibility before God; but do not carry the feeling too far. We may feel our responsibility so deeply that we may become unable to sustain it. It may cripple our joy and make slaves of us. Do not take an exaggerated view of what the Lord expects of you. He will not blame you for not doing that which is beyond your mental power or physical strength. You are required to be faithful, but you are not bound to be successful. You are to teach, but you cannot compel people to learn. You are to make things plain, but you cannot give carnal men an understanding of spiritual things. We are not the Father, nor the Savior, nor the Comforter of the Church. We cannot take the responsibility of the universe upon our shoulders."[501]

The remedy for discouragement? Spurgeon from experience says, "The iron bolt which so mysteriously fastens the door of hope and holds our spirits in gloomy prison needs a heavenly hand to push it back; and when that hand is seen, we cry with the apostle, 'Blessed be God, even the Father of our Lord Jesus Christ, the Father of mercies, and the God of all comfort; who comforteth us in all our tribulation, that we may be able to comfort them which are in any trouble, by the comfort wherewith we ourselves are comforted of God.' Simon sinks till Jesus takes him by the hand. When we are ridden with horrible fears and weighed down with intolerable incubus, we need but the Son of Righteousness to rise, and the evils generated of our darkness are driven away; but nothing short of this will chase away the nightmare of the soul.'"[502]

When thou art dry, go to thy God, ask him to pour some joy down thee, and then thou wilt get more joy up from thine own heart.

Charles Spurgeon

In *Morning and Evening,* Spurgeon advises the despondent, "You have heard it said that when a pump is dry, you must pour water down it first of all, and then you will get some up. So, Christian, when thou art dry, go to thy God, ask him to pour some joy down thee, and then thou wilt get more joy up from thine own heart."[503] And another entry said, "Your emptiness is but the preparation for your being filled, and your casting down is but the making ready for your lifting up."[504]

Never be discouraged; trust the Father's word.
In the time of trial, let His voice be heard.
Trusting in His promise, tho' the waiting long,
He will surely bless us—praise Him with a song.
~ J. H. Fillmore (1881)

In the sermon "Beauty for Ashes," Spurgeon states, "Come, my brethren, are any of you down; are you almost beneath the enemy's foot?…Think what Jesus has given you: your sins are pardoned for His name's sake; your Heaven is made secure to you, and all that is wanted to bring you there; you have grace in your hearts, and glory awaits you; you have already grace within you, and greater grace shall be granted you; you are renewed by the Spirit of Christ in your inner man, the good work is begun, and God will never leave it till he has finished it; your names are in His book, nay, graven on the palms of His hands; His love never changes; His power never diminishes; His grace never fails; His truth is firm as the hills; and His faithfulness is like the great mountains. Lean on the love of His heart, on the might of His arm, on the merit of His blood, on the power of His plea and the indwelling of His Spirit."[505]

25

The Preacher's Jealousy

"Self-love is, no doubt, the usual foundation of human jealousy…the fear lest another should by any means supplant us."[506] ~ C. H. Spurgeon

A hundred years ago Clovis Chappell said, "It is a very human trait in us to feel that another's advancement is in some way a blow to ourselves. It is equally a human trait to feel that another's downfall and disgrace in some way adds a bit of luster to our own crowns. Of course, nothing could be more utterly false."[507] *Baker's Evangelical Dictionary* defines envy as the "sin of jealousy over the blessings and achievements of others, especially the spiritual enjoyment and advance of the kingdom of Christ freely and graciously bestowed upon the people of God." Vine says that "envy differs from jealousy in that the former desires merely to deprive another of what he has, whereas the latter desires as well to have the same, or a similar, thing for itself."

Out of jealousy, Saul sought to kill David (1 Samuel 18:7–9) and Joseph's brothers did him grave harm (Genesis 37:11–35). Saith Warren Wiersbe, "There is no place for competition in the work of God, unless we are competing against sin and Satan. When we see words like *best, fastest growing, biggest, finest* applied to Christian ministries, we wonder who's getting the glory. This does not mean that it is wrong to keep records. Spurgeon used to say, 'Those who criticize statistics usually have none to report.' But we must be careful that we are not making others look bad just to make ourselves look good. And we should be able to look at the achievements and blessings of others as if they were our own."[508]

Yet he was jealous, though he did not show it,
For jealousy dislikes the world to know it.
Lord Byron

Ministerial jealousy lurks among even the greatest of preachers though often not shown. It's as Lord Byron stated, "Yet he was jealous, though he did not show it, for jealousy dislikes the world to know it." In his book *Come Before Winter*, Chuck Swindoll says, "Like an anger-blind, half-starved rat prowling in the foul-smelling sewers below street level, so is the person caged within the suffocating radius of selfish jealousy. Trapped by resentment…he feeds on the filth of his own imagination."[509]

Oscar Wilde says, "The Devil…was once crossing the Libyan Desert, and he came upon a spot where a number of small fiends were tormenting a holy hermit. The sainted man easily shook off their evil suggestions. The Devil watched their failure, and then he stepped forward to give them a lesson. [Speaking to the fiends, he said,] 'What you do is too crude.…Permit me for one moment.' [The Devil went over close to the holy man and whispered in his ear], 'Your brother has just been made [the] Bishop of Alexandria.' A scowl of malignant jealousy at once clouded the serene face of the hermit. 'That,' said the Devil to his imps, 'is the sort of thing which I should recommend.'"[510] And the Devil's legions of demons certainly employ it in their effort to destroy the preacher.

You cannot commit a greater crime against some people than to be more useful than they are. If you outrun others do not reckon upon smiles, but count upon black looks.
Charles Spurgeon

Jonathan Edwards wrote, "Some persons are always ready to level those above them down to themselves, while they are never willing to level those below them up to their own position. But he that is under the influence of true humility will avoid both these extremes. On the one hand, he will be willing that all should rise just so far as their diligence and worth of character entitle them to; and on the other hand, he will be willing that his superiors should be known and acknowledged in their place, and have rendered to them all the honors that are their due."[511] Saith Spurgeon, "You cannot commit a greater crime against some people than to be more useful than they are. If you outrun others, do not reckon upon smiles, but count upon black looks."[512]

Paul admonishes, "Don't compare yourself with others. Just look at your own work to see if you have done anything to be proud of" (Galatians 6:4 ERV). On a similar note, Vance Havner states if there was an eleventh commandment, it would be, "Thou shalt not compare." Comparison usually either breeds pride or jealousy.

Spurgeon observes, "How often, if one Christian brother does a little more than his fellow-workers, they begin to find fault with him; and if one is blessed with greater success than others are, how frequently that success is disparaged and spoken of slightingly! This spirit of envy is, more or less, *in us all,* and though perhaps we are not exhibiting it just now, it only needs a suitable opportunity for its display, and it would be manifested. No man here has any idea of how bad he really is. You do not know how good the grace of God can make you, nor how bad you are by nature, nor how bad you might become if that nature were left to itself."[513]

In the sermon "Communion with Christ and His People," Spurgeon asserts, "Are we at once glad because another prospers? If another star outshines ours, do we delight in its radiance? When we meet a brother with ten talents, do we congratulate ourselves on having such a man given to help us, or do we belittle him as much as we can? Such is the depravity of our nature that we do not readily rejoice in the progress of others if they leave us behind, but we must school ourselves to this. *A man will readily sit down and sympathize with a friend's griefs, but if he sees him honored and esteemed, he is apt to regard him as a rival and does not readily rejoice with him. This ought not to be.* Without effort we ought to be happy in our brother's happiness. If we are ill, may this be our comfort, that many are in robust health; if we are faint, let us be glad that others are strong in the Lord. By this we shall enjoy a happy fellowship like that of the perfected above."[514]

The great pastor and theologian F. B. Meyer testified of a time when he was tempted to be jealous and how it was thwarted. "It was easy," he said, "to pray for the success of G. Campbell Morgan when he was in America. But when he came back to England and took a church near mine, it was something different. The old Adam in me was inclined to jealousy, but I got up my heel upon his head and whether I felt right toward my friend, I determined to act right. My church gave a reception for him, and I acknowledged that if it was not necessary for me to preach Sunday evenings I would dearly love to go and hear him myself. Well, that made me feel right towards him. But just see how the Lord helped me out of my difficulty. There was Thomas Spurgeon [his father, Charles, had died] preaching wonderfully on one side of me. He and Mr. Morgan were so popular and drew such crowds that our church caught the overflow, and we had all we could accommodate."[515] Note, it was to this spiritual giant, that battled jealousy, that Spurgeon paid one of the greatest commendations one may give: "Meyer preaches as a man who has seen God face to face."[516]

In the aftermath of the battle of the Marathon, all of Athens were raving about Miltiades, the victorious general. Themistocles was so jealous that he shut himself up to avoid hearing the jeers about his rival. Plutarch recounts, "Yes, he got no rest day nor night; neither would he frequent festivals nor keep company with friends." Upon being asked what was wrong, Themistocles replied, "Miltiades' victory would not let me sleep."[517] He couldn't stand to see another given a place greater than his in the kingdom. Only Heaven knows how many preachers are restless over the success or position of another.

"The cure for envy [and jealousy]," says Spurgeon, "lies in living under a constant sense of the divine presence, worshiping God and communing with Him all the day long, however long the day may seem. True religion lifts the soul into a higher region, where the judgment becomes more clear and the desires are more elevated. The more of Heaven there is in our lives, the less of earth we shall covet. The fear of God casts out envy of men."[518] Act like a Jonathan to the David that "outshines" or even supplants you. Love him; don't be jealous of him.

In the sermon "Rest," Spurgeon exclaims, "Have you never heard of the Persian king who gave his various councilors different gifts. To one he gave a golden goblet, but to another a kiss; whereupon all the councilors of the court were envious of the man who had the kiss, and they counted the goblets of gold, and jewels and caskets of silver, to be less than nothing as compared with that familiar token of royal favor. O poor but favored saints, you will never envy those who quaff golden cups of fortune if you obtain the kiss from Jesus' mouth; for you know that His love is better than all the world besides, and the enjoyment of it will yield you richest rest. How can you feel the miseries of envy when you possess in Christ the best of all portions? Who wants cisterns by the river? Who cries for pebbles when he possesses pearls? The grace of faith, moreover, works in us resignation. He who fully trusts his God becomes perfectly resigned to his Father's will; he knows that all God's dealings must be right, since the Lord is much too wise to err and much too full of lovingkindness to deal harshly with his people."[519] Let the preacher say, "Amen and amen."

26
The Preacher's Weakness

"You and I may be very weak at this time, but we can be made strong out of just such weakness. We need not wish to have any strength of our own, for by faith we can reach to any degree of power in the Lord! We can have all imaginable strength for the grandest achievements desirable, if we have faith in God."[520] ~ C. H. Spurgeon

Some years ago, John Stott wrote, "It seems that the only preaching God honors, through which His wisdom and power are expressed, is the preaching of a man who is willing, in himself, to be both a weakling and a fool. God not only chooses weak and foolish people to save, but weak and foolish preachers through whom to save them—or at least preachers who are content to be weak and seem foolish in the eyes of the world."[521] "Mark the fact," J. G. Gregory says, "that the Lord uses instruments that are remarkable for their weakness."[522]

Paul knew ministerial weakness, stating, "When I am weak, then I am strong" (2 Corinthians 12:10 NIV). See Romans 7:19 and Hebrews 11:34. The more the faints and fails, troubles and trials, sorrows and sufferings, the more divine strength was imparted to him. Paul's feebleness was the foundation of his powerfulness.

John Gill, pastor at the Metropolitan Tabernacle from 1720–1771, says "he was not only able to sustain the conflict, but became more than a conqueror, and even to triumph in the midst of these adversities."[523] "Paul's weaknesses," comments J. M. Harris, "provided him with the opportunity to experience Christ's power (2 Corinthians 12:9b), that he could even take pleasure in them."[524]

"A primary qualification," states Spurgeon, "for serving God with any amount of success and for doing God's work well and triumphantly is a sense of our own weakness."[525] Further, he asserts, "The best man here, if he knows what he is, knows that he is out of his depth in his sacred calling. We are weak, exceedingly weak, every one of us. We must work miracles by Divine power, or else be total failures."[526]

Spurgeon knew himself to be weak apart from God. D. L. Moody said of him, "He is as weak as any other man apart from his Lord. Moses was nothing, but Moses' God was almighty. Samson was nothing when he lost his strength; but when it came back to him, he was a mighty man; and so, dear friends, bear in mind that, if we can just link our weakness to God's strength, we can go forth and be a blessing in the world."[527]

Spurgeon, realizing his weakness to preach, would physically become sick and tormented with terrible fear prior to preaching. He testifies, "For many, many years, my own preaching was exceedingly painful to me because of the fears which beset me before entering the pulpit. Often, my dread of facing the people has been overwhelming. Even the physical feeling, which came of the mental emotion, has been painful, but this weakness has been an education for me."[528]

Spurgeon wrote to his grandfather regarding the terrible fears and sickness before preaching. The aged minister replied, "I have been preaching for sixty years, and I still feel many tremblings. Be content to have it so; for when your emotion goes away, your strength will be gone."[529] Saith Spurgeon, "When we preach and think nothing of it, the people think nothing of it, and God does nothing by it. An overwhelming sense of weakness should not be regarded as an evil, but should be accepted as helpful to the true minister of Christ."[530] *"I believe that, when we preach in conscious weakness, it adds a wonderful force to the words we utter."*[531]

In the sermon "God's Cure for Man's Weakness," Spurgeon states, "The church's [preachers, Christians at large] weakness springs mainly and mostly from a want of faith in her God and in the revelation which God has entrusted to her. When men believe intensely, they act vigorously, and when their principles penetrate their very souls and become precious to them as life itself, then no suffering is too severe and no undertaking is too laborious and no conflict too heroic. They will enter upon impossibilities, laugh at them, and overcome them, when once they know of a surety that the principles which move them are most certainly from God."[532]

In our weaknesses, we cry, "Who is sufficient for these

things?" (2 Corinthians 2:16). Our answer is that of Paul and Spurgeon: "My sufficiency is of God." As Vincent says, "Real strength comes only out of that weakness which, distrustful of itself, gives itself up to God."[533] Saith Spurgeon, "He asks your weakness. He has none of that Himself, and He is longing, therefore, to take your weakness and use it as the instrument in His own mighty hand. Will you not yield your weakness to Him and receive His strength?"[534]

> Oh! 'twas a cheering word indeed—
> Exactly suited to my need!
> 'Sufficient for thee is my grace;
> Thy weakness my great power displays.'
>
> Now I despond and mourn no more;
> I welcome all I feared before.
> Though weak, I'm strong; tho' troubled, blest,
> For Christ's own power shall on me rest.
>
> ~ John Newton (1799)

Note, Spurgeon states, "SOME kinds of weakness are of God's appointment and necessarily incident to manhood; they are not sinful, and therefore we may continue to be subject to them without regret. There is another kind of weakness which is sinful, a weakness which springs not from nature but from fallen nature, not from God's appointment, but from our sinfulness; and out of this [neglect of prayer and intake of the Word, slothfulness, carnality, lack of dependence upon the Holy Spirit, etc.], we should desire to be delivered. We cannot pray for strength in sinful weakness, but must earnestly plead for strength to come out of it and to be made strong. It is the inestimable privilege of many a Christian to be strong in weakness when the weakness is only one of infirmity [hardship, trial], but it is an equally precious boon to be made strong out of weakness when that weakness is of a sinful kind."[535] God enables both.

At age nineteen Spurgeon wrote a hymn for the celebration of the jubilee services at Waterbeach on June 26, 1853. Every stanza states a reason for persevering in the work divinely assigned: God's love, Word, Grace, Presence, Name, and Hope of Heaven. (These and other incentives for Paul's and Spurgeon's ministerial endurance through grave adversity are examined in Volume 2 of this set.)

When once I mourned a load of sin,
When conscience felt a wound within,
When all my works were thrown away,
When on my knees I knelt to pray,
Then, blissful hour remembered well,
I learnt Thy love, Immanuel!

When storms of sorrow toss my soul,
When waves of care around me roll,
When comforts sink, when joys shall flee,
When hopeless gulfs shall gape for me,
One word the tempest's rage shall quell—
That word, Thy name, Immanuel.

When for the truth I suffer shame,
When foes pour scandal on Thy name,
When cruel taunts and jeers abound,
When "bulls of Bashan" gird me round,
Secure within my tower I'll dwell—
That tower, Thy grace, Immanuel.

When Hell, enraged, lifts up her roar,
When Satan stops my path before,
When fiends rejoice and wait my end,
When legion'd hosts their arrows send,
Fear not, my soul, but hurl at Hell
Thy battle-cry, Immanuel.

When down the hill of life I go,
When o'er my feet death's waters flow,
When in the deep'ning flood I sink,
When friends stand weeping on the brink,
I'll mingle with my last farewell
Thy lovely name, Immanuel.

When tears are banished from mine eye,
When fairer worlds than these are nigh,
When Heaven shall fill my ravished sight,
When I shall bathe in sweet delight,
One joy all joys shall far excel—
To see Thy face, Immanuel.

Appendix 1
Spurgeon's Weekly Schedule

Spurgeon's weekly schedule, sifted from his autobiography *The Full Harvest*[536]

Monday

Wake early / devotional time (Spurgeon said, "It is a good rule never to look into the face of a man in the morning till you have looked into the face of God, and equally a good rule always to have business with Heaven [private prayer] before you have any business with earth."[537])

Revise yesterday's sermon (top priority)

Reading of letters (J. W. Harrald, his secretary, opened and arranged for speedy answers)

Dictating of letters / a weekly average of five hundred letters to be answered[538]

Late afternoon, send the completed revision of the Sunday sermon to the printer

5:30 p.m.–7:00 p.m., meeting with the elders or preside at the first part of the prayer meeting at the church/preach

8:30 p.m., conclude prayer meeting / interviews with guests and church member candidates or inquirers (On some Monday nights an extra service was squeezed in at a neighboring church at 8:00 p.m.)

Tuesday

Wake early / devotional time

Work on the second draft of Sunday's sermon revision

11:00 a.m., send the revised second draft of the Sunday sermon to the printer

11:00 a.m.–1:00 p.m., reply to letters and engage in pressing literary work

3:00 p.m., counsel inquirers and hold interviews with church candidates

5:00 p.m.–5:30 p.m., a brief break for tea / converse with helpers about those interviewed

5:30 p.m., resume interviews until completed / preside at the annual meeting of a Tabernacle society or charity

Wednesday

Wake early / devotional time

Take mid-week Sabbath / J. W. Harrald to keep the schedule clear on this day

Family time with Susannah and the twins

Take a long drive into the country / refuel mentally and spiritually

Thursday

Wake early / devotional time

Do correspondence / literary work (*The Treasury of the Psalms,* etc.)

Final review of sermon draft for publication / send proof to the printer for publication

Time and weather permitting, retire to my summer house in the garden to write

After dinner, prepare for tonight's sermon ("The den" was his secret retirement place for study and prayer where the sermon was prepared with the research assistance of one of his secretaries.)

6:00 p.m.–7:00 p.m., prayer meeting in the lecture hall for the night's service

7:00 p.m.–8:00 p.m., preach

At the close of service, meet with various hearers waiting to talk

Friday

Wake early / devotional time

Prepare lecture for the Pastors' College

3:00 p.m.–5:00 p.m., lecture at the Pastors' College

5:00 p.m.–6:00 p.m. (or longer), meet with students upon their request

Preach a sermon, observe communion with students (occasionally)

If no other obligation, like the anniversary meeting of the evening classes, or preaching engagement, or sick person to visit, head for home

Saturday

Wake early / devotional time

Meet with my secretary to finish work of the week / correspondence

Interview applicants for the Pastors' College / dictate letters regarding the decision of the applicant's acceptance or rejection

Write magazine articles, read books for reviews in *The Sword and the Trowel*

Spend time in the garden with Susannah, and / or special friends

Visitors welcome at Westwood / tea table of fellowship

Family worship in study

6:00 p.m., bid guests good-bye

Prepare tomorrow's morning sermon / get Susannah to read aloud various reference works selected until the outline develops / sketch the outline on a half-sheet of notebook paper

Initiate preparation of the Sabbath's evening sermon / select text and the general notion of lessons to be drawn from it / wait until tomorrow afternoon to fully develop it

Sunday

Wake early / devotional time

Arrive at the Tabernacle thirty minutes before service

Select hymns for service

Prayer meeting with deacons / elders

11:00 a.m., punctually enter church to start the service

Preach, no briefer than 43 minutes, but no longer than 45 minutes

Conduct informal reception with friends

Dinner (lunch), eat / abide with friends close to the church in the afternoon due to the long drive home to Westwood / visit the sick (Spurgeon's nine-acre estate [see note in the endnote] housed cows, horses, pigs, dogs, sheep, turkeys, ducks, geese, and pigeons, and "he took interest in them all."[539] It also had a lake and was home to his magnificent garden.)

4:00 p.m., prepare for tonight's evangelistic sermon (its idea already simmering)

Evening, see an inquirer or a candidate for church membership

6:00 p.m., preach

Observe communion, except on the second Sunday of the month

Counsel with those seeking salvation, if not too weary / exhausted

Go home

Note: Not cited are all of Spurgeon's additional preaching engagements throughout the week outside the Tabernacle ("Spurgeon's services were constantly in request every day or hour that was not required to meet the claims of his pastorate."[540]) and the time slots spent reading six books a week. Meal times, for the most part, are excluded due to the absence of data.

Appendix 2
Resources for the Preacher

Publications by Frank Shivers to assist the minister.

Evangelistic Preaching 101

The Evangelistic Invitation 101

Revivals 101

The Minister and the Funeral

Basics of Biblical Praying

How to Preach Without Evangelistic Results
   (Pamphlet & DVD)

Exposition of the Psalms (Three Volumes)

Life Principles from Proverbs

Spurs to Soul Winning

Evangelistic Praying

[1] Spurgeon, C. H. "Three Names High on the Muster-Roll." Sermon delivered August 16, 1891, Metropolitan Tabernacle.

[2] Spurgeon, C. H. *Lectures to My Students.* (Grand Rapids: Zondervan Publishing House, 1954), 161–162.

[3] Spurgeon, C. H. "Christ's Loneliness and Ours." Sermon published August 8, 1907, Metropolitan Tabernacle.

[4] Spurgeon, C. H. *Autobiography,* Volume 2: *The Full Harvest 1860–1892.* (Carlisle, PA: The Banner of Truth Trust, 1973), [v]; and "Christ's Dying Word for His Church." Sermon delivered November 3, 1889, Metropolitan Tabernacle.

[5] Spurgeon, C. H. "Christ's Dying Word for His Church." Sermon delivered November 3, 1889, Metropolitan Tabernacle.

[6] Spurgeon, C. H. *Lectures to My Students: Addresses Delivered to the Students of the Pastors' College, Metropolitan Tabernacle. Second series.* (Vol. 2). (New York: Robert Carter and Brothers, 1889), 46.

[7] Spurgeon, C. H. *The Salt-cellars: Being a Collection of Proverbs, Together with Homely Notes Thereon.* (1889), 89.

[8] Spurgeon, C. H. *The Full Harvest,* 194.

[9] Spurgeon, C. H. *Faith's Checkbook,* Preface.

[10] Carlile, J. C. *C. H. Spurgeon: An Interpretative Biography.* (London: The Religious Tract Society and The Kingsgate Press, 1934), 305.

[11] Spurgeon, C. H. "Christ's Dying Word for His Church." Sermon delivered November 3, 1889, Metropolitan Tabernacle.

[12] Spurgeon, C. H. "Watching to See." Sermon delivered January 26, 1882, Metropolitan Tabernacle.

[13] Spurgeon, *The Full Harvest,* Flyleaf.

[14] Peabody, A. P. "Spurgeon," *North American Review,* 86 (1858), 275.

[15] Hayden, Eric W. "Charles H. Spurgeon: A Gallery of Famous Friends." https://www.christianitytoday.com/history/issues/issue-29/charles-h-spurgeon-gallery-of-famous-friends.html, accessed December 9, 2022.

[16] Spurgeon, Susannah and William Harrald. *Autobiography Diary, Letters, and Records,* Vol. 1, 71.

[17] Data drawn from the Artillery Street Evangelical Church website. https://artillery-street.org.uk/index.php/about-us/history/, accessed December 24, 2022.

[18] *Spurgeon's Autobiography,* Volume 1. (Chicago, New York, Toronto: Fleming H. Revell Company, 1898), 151.

19 Ibid., 135. (May 5 entry in his diary).

20 *Spurgeon's Autobiography,* "A Good Confession," Chapter 14, 152.

21 Spurgeon, Susannah and William Harrald. *Autobiography Diary, Letters, and Records,* Vol. 1, 135.

22 Ibid., 190.

23 Spurgeon, C. H. "The First Sermon in the Tabernacle." Sermon delivered March 25, 1861, Metropolitan Tabernacle.

24 Spurgeon, C. H. "Under Arrest." Sermon delivered March 3, 1887, Metropolitan Tabernacle.

25 Spurgeon, C. H. "The Truth of God's Salvation." Sermon delivered February 16, 1888, Metropolitan Tabernacle.

26 Spurgeon, C. H. "Healing for the Wounded." Sermon delivered November 11, 1855, New Park Street Chapel.

27 Spurgeon, Susannah and William Harrald. *Autobiography Diary, Letters, and Records,* Vol. 1, 406.

28 Charles H. Spurgeon. "A Baptist Page Portrait." https://www.wholesomewords.org/biography/biospurgeon6.html, accessed December 19, 2022.

29 Fullerton, W. Y. *Charles H. Spurgeon, Biography,* 121.

30 Ibid., 121–122.

31 Day, Richard E. *The Shadow of the Broad Brim,* (Judson Press), 179.

32 Ibid., 122.

33 Ibid., 124.

34 Williams, W. *Personal Reminiscences of Charles Haddon Spurgeon.* (London: The Religious Tract Society, 1895), 17.

35 Ibid., 18.

36 Fullerton, W. Y. *Charles H. Spurgeon, Biography,* 120.

37 Ibid.

38 Ross, Bob. *A Pictorial Biography of C. H. Spurgeon,* 70–71.

39 Spurgeon, C. H. *The Full Harvest,* 313.

40 Williams, W. *Personal Reminiscences of Charles Haddon Spurgeon.* (London: The Religious Tract Society, 1895), 13.

41 Fullerton, W. Y. "The Apprentice Preacher." http://www.reformedreader.org/rbb/spurgeon/fullerton/bioch03.htm accessed December 20, 2022.

42 Ibid.

43 Spurgeon, C. H. *C. H. Spurgeon's Autobiography, Compiled from His Diary, Letters, and Records, by His Wife and His Private Secretary, 1834–*

1854, vol. 1. (Cincinnati; Chicago; St. Louis: Curts & Jennings, 1898), 200–201.

[44] Ibid.

[45] Spurgeon, Susannah and William Harrald. *Autobiography Diary, Letters, and Records,* Vol. 1, 269.

[46] Drummond, Lewis. *Spurgeon: Prince of Preachers.* (Grand Rapids: Kregel Publications, 1992), 195.

[47] Spurgeon, Susannah and William Harrald. *Autobiography Diary, Letters, and Records,* Vol. 1, 380.

[48] Fullerton, W. Y. *A Word Portrait.*

[49] "Charles Haddon Spurgeon," in *20 Centuries of Great Preaching: An Encyclopedia of Preaching,* 12 vols., edited by Clyde E. Fant, Jr. and William M. Pinson, Jr. (Waco, TX: Word Books, 1971), VI/3.

[50] Spurgeon, C. H. *The Full Harvest,* 37.

[51] Spurgeon, C. H. "The First Sermon in the Tabernacle." Sermon delivered March 25, 1861, Metropolitan Tabernacle.

[52] Hayden, Eric W. "Charles H. Spurgeon: Did You Know?," https://www.christianitytoday.com/history/issues/issue-29/charles-h-spurgeon-did-you-know.html, accessed November 19, 2022.

[53] Ibid.

[54] Day, Richard E. *The Shadow of the Broad Brim.* (Judson Press), 99.

[55] "Charles Haddon Spurgeon," in *20 Centuries of Great Preaching: An Encyclopedia of Preaching,* 12 vols., edited by Clyde E. Fant, Jr. and William M. Pinson, Jr. (Waco, TX: Word Books, 1971), VI/3.

[56] Spurgeon, C. H. "Special Protracted Prayer." Sermon Delivered March 1, 1868, Metropolitan Tabernacle.

[57] Spurgeon, C. H. "The Cause and Cure of Weariness in Sunday School Teachers." Sermon Delivered November 8, 1877, Metropolitan Tabernacle.

[58] Hayden, Eric W. (former Pastor at Metropolitan Tabernacle). Cited in the *Christian History Magazine,* Issue 29, 1991, 2–3.

[59] Hayden, Eric W. "Charles H. Spurgeon: Did You Know?," https://www.christianitytoday.com/history/issues/issue-29/charles-h-spurgeon-did-you-know.html, accessed November 19, 2022.

[60] Spurgeon, C. H. *C. H. Spurgeon's Autobiography, Compiled from His Diary, Letters, and Records, by His Wife and His Private Secretary, 1834–1854,* vol. 2. (Cincinnati; Chicago; St. Louis: Curts & Jennings, 1898), 6.

[61] Hayden, Eric W.
https://christianhistoryinstitute.org/magazine/article/spurgeon-did-you-know, accessed December 28, 2022.

[62] "Mr. Spurgeon at the Agricultural Hall," *The Sword and the Trowel,* 1867.

[63] Thomas Spurgeon. THE BURNING OF THE METROPOLITAN TABERNACLE. Metropolitan Tabernacle Pulpit, Vol 44.

[64] Carroll, B. H. "The Death of Spurgeon," an address delivered in Nashville, Tennessee, February, 1892, in *Sermons and Life Sketch of B. H. Carroll, D.D.,* compiled by J. B. Cranfill (Philadelphia: The American Baptist Publication Society, 1893), 29.

[65] Henry, Carl F. H. in the foreword to Lewis Drummond, *Spurgeon: Prince of Preachers*.

[66] The address was first delivered on April 25, 1934; a capacity crowd swelled the Royal Albert Hall, London.

[67] Cited in Lewis Drummond, *Spurgeon: Prince of Preachers*, 25.

[68] Fullerton, W. Y. *Charles H. Spurgeon, Biography,* Chapter 14.

[69] Ibid., Chapter 10.

[70] *Sword and Trowel,* (1889), 551; quoted in L. R. Bush and T. J. Nettles. *Baptists and the Bible.* (Chicago: Moody, 1980), 251.

[71] Spurgeon, C. H. "Preach the Gospel." Sermon delivered August 5, 1855, New Park Street Chapel.

[72] "Charles Haddon Spurgeon—A Passion for Preaching, Part Three," Wednesday, September 22, 2004. Albert Mohler.com, accessed December 19, 2022.

[73] Spurgeon, C. H. "Justification and Glory." Sermon delivered April 30, 1865, Metropolitan Tabernacle.

[74] *The Sword and Trowel,* (1891), 446. This statement concluded: "Our hope is the Personal Premillennial Return of the Lord." Lewis A. Drummond in his biography of Spurgeon states, "Spurgeon confessed to be a premillennialist."

[75] George, Christian. Beeson Podcast, Episode 383. March 13, 2018.

[76] Spurgeon, Susannah and William Harrald. *Autobiography Diary, Letters, and Records,* Vol. 1, 408.

[77] Ibid.

[78] Packer, J. I. *Psalms,* Volume II, Introduction.

[79] Ibid.

[80] From the "Monthly Record of the Free Church of Scotland," August 1958.

81 Drummond, Lewis. *Spurgeon: Prince of Preachers*. (Grand Rapids: Kregel Publications, 1992), 215.

82 *From the Pulpit to the Palm-Branch*. (London: Passmore & Alabaster, 1892), 34.

83 Ray, Charles. *A Marvelous Ministry: The Story of C. H. Spurgeon's Sermons, 1855–1905*. (1905), Chapter 9.

84 The Lost Sermons of C. H. Spurgeon—399 sermons—February 1851 to Autumn 1854; The New Park Street Pulpit—347 sermons—January 1855 to November 1860; The Metropolitan Tabernacle Pulpit—3,216 sermons—December 1860 to January 1892. Cited in *The Lost Sermons of C. H. Spurgeon*, Volume 7. (B & H Publishers, 2022), 9.

85 www.grace-ebooks.com

86 Ray, Charles. *The Complete Works of C. H. Spurgeon,* Volume 71: A Marvelous Ministry, (1905).

87 Ibid.

88 This number is cited by The Spurgeon Center for Biblical Preaching at Midwestern Seminary. Cited in "How Spurgeon Scheduled His Week", June 27, 2017. https://www.spurgeon.org/resource-library/blog-entries/how-spurgeon-scheduled-his-week/, accessed January 4, 2023.

89 Spurgeon, C. H. "Watching to See." Sermon delivered January 26, 1882.

90 Spurgeon. *An All Round Ministry*, 272.

91 Rhodes, Ray, Jr. "Follow Spurgeon's Example in Reading Good Books." March 14, 2017.

92 Wright, William. *The Wit and Wisdom of Rev. Charles H. Spurgeon*. (Baltimore: R.H. Woodward Company, 1894), 4.

93 Hayden, Eric W. "Charles H. Spurgeon: Did You Know?," https://christianhistoryinstitute.org/magazine/article/spurgeon-did-you-know, accessed November 22, 2022.

94 Fullerton, W. Y. *Charles H. Spurgeon, Biography,* A Bundle of Opinions, Chapter 14.

95 Spurgeon. The Full Harvest, 498.

96 Spurgeon, C. H. *Morning and Evening,* August 21 (Morning).

97 Spurgeon, C. H. "Black Clouds and Bright Blessings." Sermon delivered at the Metropolitan Tabernacle, published September 15, 1910.

98 Carlile, J. C. *C. H. Spurgeon: An Interpretative Biography*. (London: The Religious Tract Society and The Kingsgate Press, 1934), 299.

99 "4 Reasons Spurgeon Died Poor," October 11, 2016. The Spurgeon Center at Midwestern Seminary. https://www.spurgeon.org/resource-

library/blog-entries/4-reasons-spurgeon-died-poor/, accessed January 6, 2023.

[100] Ibid.

[101] Spurgeon, C. H. "The Serpent's Sentence." Sermon delivered September 21, 1890, Metropolitan Tabernacle.

[102] Dallimore. *Spurgeon: A Biography,* 143. Spurgeon's generosity cited is heartwarming. On his 25th anniversary the deacons gave him $753,943.68; he gave $579,421.00 of it to the almshouses alone. *Note*: The Pastors' College began with Spurgeon's instruction of one student, Thomas Medhurst. A year later a second student was added. In the school's first five years 15 students were trained. Spurgeon's College gives the founding year as 1857, other timelines state 1858, but Spurgeon in his autobiography refers to its beginning "five or six years ago" in a message on May 19, 1861 (*The Full Harvest,* 97).

[103] "4 Reasons Spurgeon Died Poor," October 11, 2016. The Spurgeon Center at Midwestern Seminary. https://www.spurgeon.org/resource-library/blog-entries/4-reasons-spurgeon-died-poor/, accessed January 6, 2023.

[104] Dallimore. *Spurgeon: A Biography,* 104.

[105] Spurgeon. *Lectures to My Students,* Vol. 1, preface.

[106] Spurgeon, *The Full Harvest,* 97.

[107] Spurgeon, C. H. *Lectures to My Students: Commenting and Commentaries; Lectures Addressed to the Students of the Pastors' College, Metropolitan Tabernacle,* (Vol. 4). (New York: Sheldon & Company, 1876), 6.

[108] Spurgeon, C. H. *Autobiography, Volume 2: The Full Harvest 1860–1892.* (Carlisle, PA: The Banner of Truth Trust, 1973), Flyleaf.

[109] Adkins, Jason. "The Rise and Fall of Spurgeon's College." January 19, 2010. https://standingonshoulders.wordpress.com/2010/01/19/the-rise-and-fall-of-spurgeons-college/, accessed January 8, 2023.

[110] Ibid.

[111] Johnson, Thomas. *Twenty-Eight Years a Slave,* 88.

[112] Hoover, Christine. "Charles Spurgeon's Unlikely Friend." September 11, 2017. https://www.thegospelcoalition.org/reviews/steal-away-home-charles-spurgeon/, accessed January 16, 2023. No documentation was cited in this article outside of a book written in 2017.

[113] "Michael Kenneth Nicholls (vice-principal of Spurgeon's College). Spurgeon's College."

https://www.christianitytoday.com/history/issues/issue-29/spurgeons-college.html, accessed January 18, 2023.

[114] White, B. R. *The Baptist Quarterly.* "Charles Haddon Spurgeon: Educationalist. Part 2: The Principles and Practice of the Pastors' College," 87. https://biblicalstudies.org.uk/pdf/bq/32-2_073.pdf, accessed January 8, 2023.

[115] Spurgeon, C. H. *Autobiography, Volume 2: The Full Harvest 1860–1892.* (Carlisle, PA: The Banner of Truth Trust, 1973), 162.

[116] Ibid., 161.

[117] Ibid., 161–164.

[118] https://spurgeons.org/about-us/our-heritage/, accessed January 8, 2023.

[119] "Spurgeon and the Metropolitan Tabernacle." https://www.elephantandcastle.org.uk/a-brief-history/metropolitan-tabernacle/, accessed January 9, 2023.

[120] Hayden, Eric W. "Did You Know?" *Christian History Magazine,* Issue 29, 1991, 2–3.

[121] Ulmer, Selah. "3 Things You Didn't Know About Spurgeon's Wife," October 17, 2017. https://www.spurgeon.org/resource-library/blog-entries/3-things-you-didnt-know-about-spurgeons-wife/, accessed November 19, 2022.

[122] Spurgeon, *Autobiography,* Vol. 1, 188.

[123] DiPrima, Alex and Geof Chang. "Charles Spurgeon, Women's Ministry, and Female Preachers," December 11, 2019.

[124] Ibid.

[125] Rhodes, Ray. *Susie: The Life and Legacy of Susannah Spurgeon, Wife of Charles H. Spurgeon.* (Chicago: Moody Publishers, 2018).

[126] Ibid.

[127] Spurgeon. *The Full Harvest,* 71.

[128] *Christian History Magazine,* Vol. 29: "The Life & Times of Charles H. Spurgeon," 1991. Cited under heading "Spurgeon's Critics."

[129] Spurgeon, Charles. *The Sword and the Trowel,* FEBRUARY, 1869.

[130] Spurgeon, C. H. "Preach the Gospel." Sermon delivered August 5, 1855, New Park Street Chapel.

[131] Fullerton, W. Y. "The Apprentice Preacher." http://www.reformedreader.org/rbb/spurgeon/fullerton/bioch03.htm, accessed December 20, 2022.

[132] Carroll, B. H. *Baptists and Their Doctrines,* edited by Timothy and Denise George, 59.

[133] *From the Pulpit to the Palm-Branch,* 30–31.

[134] Hale, Terry D. "From Mentone to Norwood: The Final Journey of C. H. Spurgeon," January 31, 2022. https://www.spurgeon.org/resource-library/blog-entries/from-mentone-to-norwood-the-final-journey-of-c-h-spurgeon/, accessed January 17, 2023.

[135] Spurgeon. *The Full Harvest,* 504.

[136] *From the Pulpit to the Palm-Branch.* (London: Passmore & Alabaster, 1893), 44.

[137] Hale, Terry D. "From Mentone to Norwood: The Final Journey of C. H. Spurgeon," January 31, 2022. https://www.spurgeon.org/resource-library/blog-entries/from-mentone-to-norwood-the-final-journey-of-c-h-spurgeon/, accessed January 17, 2023.

[138] *From the Pulpit to the Palm-Branch.* (London: Passmore & Alabaster, 1893), 95–204.

[139] Spurgeon. *The Full Harvest,* 505.

[140] Ibid.

[141] Ibid., 507.

[142] Allen, James T. *Life Story of C. H. Spurgeon,* Chapter 8: "Laying the Warrior to Rest."

[143] Fullerton, W. Y. *Charles H. Spurgeon: London's Most Popular Preacher.* (Chicago: Moody Press, 1966), 274.

[144] Spurgeon, C. H. "The Time is Short." Sermon delivered in 1874, Metropolitan Tabernacle.

[145] Spurgeon. *The Full Harvest,* 397–398.

[146] Allen, James T. *Life Story of C. H. Spurgeon,* Chapter 8: "Laying the Warrior to Rest."

[147] Carlile, J. C. *C. H. Spurgeon: An Interpretative Biography.* (London: The Religious Tract Society and The Kingsgate Press, 1934), 24.

[148] Spurgeon, Susannah and William Harrald. *Autobiography Diary, Letters, and Records,* Vol. 1, 6.

[149] Spurgeon. *Lectures to My Students,* 203.

[150] Spurgeon, C. H. "The Sound in the Mulberry Trees." Sermon delivered May 31, 1857, New Park Street Chapel.

[151] Spurgeon. *Lectures to My Students,* 39. Further he said, "When I think upon the all but infinite mischief which may result from a mistake as in our vocation for the Christian pastorate, I feel overwhelmed with fear lest any of us should be slack in examining our credentials; and I had rather that we stood too much in doubt, and examined too frequently, than that we should become cumberers of the ground."

[152] Spurgeon. *Lectures to My Students,* 26–27.

[153] Lloyd-Jones, Martin. *Preachers and Preaching.* (Zondervan, 1971), 105.

[154] Jowett. *The Preacher: His Life and Work,* 16–18.

[155] Lloyd-Jones, Martin. *On Being a Pastor.* (Moody Press, 2004), 19.

[156] Ryle, J. C. *A Self-Portrait,* 59.

[157] Spurgeon, C. H. "Preach the Gospel." Sermon delivered August 5, 1855, New Park Street Chapel.

[158] Griffith Thomas, W. H. "The Divine Call." https://img.sermonindex.net/modules/articles/article_pdf.php?aid=456 56, accessed December 7, 2022.

[159] Spurgeon, C. H. "Harvest Men Wanted." Sermon delivered August 17, 1873, Metropolitan Tabernacle.

[160] MacArthur, J., Jr. (Ed.). *The MacArthur Study Bible* (electronic ed.). (Nashville, TN: Word Pub., 1997). 1864.

[161] Spurgeon, C. H. *Feathers for Arrows.* (London: Passmore & Alabaster, 1870), 260.

[162] MacArthur, J., Jr. (Ed.). *The MacArthur Study Bible* (electronic ed.). (Nashville, TN: Word Pub., 1997). 1864.

[163] Spurgeon. *Lectures to My Students,* 32.

[164] Prime, Derek J. *On Being a Pastor.* (Moody Press, 2004), 25.

[165] Spurgeon, *Lectures to My Students,* 33.

[166] Ibid., 32.

[167] Ibid., 30.

[168] Ibid., 31.

[169] Ibid., 40.

[170] Ibid., 28–29.

[171] Ibid., 53.

[172] Griffith Thomas, W. H. "The Divine Call." https://img.sermonindex.net/modules/articles/article_pdf.php?aid=456 56, accessed December 7, 2022.

[173] Spurgeon, *Lectures to My Students,* 61.

[174] Blackaby, Henry. *Experiencing God,* 194

[175] Drummond, Lewis. *Spurgeon, Prince of Preachers.* (Grand Rapids, Kregel, 1992), 118.

[176] Spurgeon, C. H. "Saying Versus Doing." Sermon delivered May 1, 1879, Metropolitan Tabernacle.

[177] Griffith Thomas, W. H. "The Divine Call." https://img.sermonindex.net/modules/articles/article_pdf.php?aid=456 56, accessed December 7, 2022.

[178] Spurgeon. *Lectures to My Students,* 34.

[179] Ibid., 40.

[180] Kulp, George. *The Making of a Preacher:* Chapter 1: "The Preacher's Call."

[181] Hurst, John Fletcher. *John Wesley the Methodist.* (New York: Eaton & Mains, 1903), 90. http://www.books.google.com/books?id=LOJpAAAAMAAJ...(accessed June 15, 2009).

[182] Spurgeon, Charles Haddon. *All of Grace,* Chapter 3.

[183] Barnes, Albert. *Barnes Notes on the Bible,* 1 Corinthians 15:9.

[184] Truett, George W. *A Quest for Souls.* (New York, London: Harper & Brothers, Publishers, 1917), 50.

[185] Chambers, Oswald. *My Utmost for His Highest,* February 18 entry.

[186] Spurgeon, C. H. "Tearful Sowing and Joyful Reaping." Sermon delivered April 25, 1869, Metropolitan Tabernacle.

[187] Spurgeon, *Morning and Evening,* February 3 (Evening).

[188] Spurgeon, C. H. "The Minister's Trumpet Blast and Church Member's Warning." Sermon Delivered January 8, 1860, New Park Street Chapel.

[189] Spurgeon, Charles Haddon. *All of Grace*, Chapter 3.

[190] https://macarthurcenter.org/step-1-personal-preparation/, accessed November 16, 2022.

[191] Spurgeon, C. H. "Self Low, but Christ High." Sermon Delivered August 30, 1890, Metropolitan Tabernacle.

[192] Spurgeon, Charles. "Fresh Grace Confidently Expected." Sermon Delivered July 19, 1873, Metropolitan Tabernacle.

[193] Spurgeon. *Morning and Evening,* October 2 (Evening).

[194] Lloyd-Jones, Martin. *Preaching and Preachers.* (Zondervan, 1971), 264.

[195] https://www.kevinhalloran.net/the-best-timothy-keller-quotes/, accessed November 25, 2022.

[196] Exell, J. S. *The Biblical Illustrator: 1 Corinthians* (Vol. 2). (New York: Anson D. F. Randolph & Company, n.d.), 404.

[197] J. Hudson Taylor. "Faith in God's Faithfulness." http://articles.ochristian.com/article9560.shtml, accessed December 28, 2022.

[198] Spurgeon, C. H. "The Sealing of the Spirit." Sermon delivered March 19, 1876, Metropolitan Tabernacle.

[199] Spurgeon, C. H. "The Glorious Right Hand of the Lord." Sermon delivered February 24, 1861, New Park Street Chapel (the entry cites Metropolitan Tabernacle, but the first sermon wasn't delivered at that location until March 24, 1861.)

[200] Spurgeon, C. H. "The Raging Lion." Sermon delivered November 17, 1861, Metropolitan Tabernacle.

[201] Spurgeon, C. H. "The Believer Sinking in the Mire." Sermon delivered in 1865, Metropolitan Tabernacle.

[202] Spurgeon, C. H. "Is Conversion Necessary?" Sermon delivered July 19, 1874, Metropolitan Tabernacle.

[203] Ibid.

[204] Spurgeon, C. H. "The One Foundation." Sermon delivered September 14, 1879, Metropolitan Tabernacle.

[205] Spurgeon, C. H. "The Danger of Doubting." Sermon delivered March 16, 1862, Metropolitan Tabernacle.

[206] Spurgeon, C. H. *Morning and Evening.* September 23 (morning entry).

[207] Spurgeon, C. H. "Come, My Beloved!" Sermon delivered March 4, 1888, Metropolitan Tabernacle.

[208] Spurgeon, C. H. "The One Foundation." Sermon delivered September 14, 1879, Metropolitan Tabernacle.

[209] Spurgeon, C. H. "Full Assurance." Sermon delivered April 28, 1861, Metropolitan Tabernacle.

[210] Spurgeon, C. H. "Assurance Sought." *Metropolitan Tabernacle Pulpit:* Vol. 63. (London: Passmore and Alabaster, 1917; reprint, Pasadena, TX: Pilgrim Publications, 1980), 21.

[211] Rogers, Adrian. "How Do I Know I'm Saved?," http://www.christianity.com, accessed November 21, 2013.

[212] Spurgeon, C. H. "The Truth of God's Salvation." Sermon delivered February 16, 1888, Metropolitan Tabernacle.

[213] Amundsen, Darrel. "The Anguish and Agonies of Charles Spurgeon," in: *Christian History,* Issue 29, Volume X, No. 1, 23.

[214] Ibid.

[215] Spurgeon, *An All-Round Ministry.* (Carlisle, PA: Banner of Truth Trust, 1978), 159.

[216] Spurgeon, C. H. "Heart's Ease." Sermon delivered August 27, 1865, Metropolitan Tabernacle.

[217] Spurgeon, C. H. "David's Five-Stringed Harp." Sermon delivered March 27, 1884, Metropolitan Tabernacle.

[218] Spurgeon, C. H. *Lectures to My Students: Addresses Delivered to the Students of the Pastors' College, Metropolitan Tabernacle. Second Series.* (Vol. 2). (New York: Robert Carter and Brothers, 1889), 259.

[219] Ibid., 242.

[220] Spurgeon, C. H. "My Times Are in Thy Hand." Sermon delivered May 17, 1891, Metropolitan Tabernacle.

[221] Spurgeon, *The Treasury of David,* Psalm 120:1.

[222] Spurgeon, C. H. *The Treasury of David: Psalms 27–57* (Vol. 2). (London; Edinburgh; New York: Marshall Brothers, n.d.), 63.

[223] Spurgeon, *The Treasury of David,* Psalm 120:3.

[224] *The Spurgeon Study Bible*, 716.

[225] Spurgeon, C. H. *Eccentric Preachers.* (London: Passmore & Alabaster, 1879), 5.

[226] Spurgeon, C. H. "Our Hiding Place." Sermon delivered November 11, 1877, Metropolitan Tabernacle.

[227] Spurgeon, C. H. "Whither Goest Thou?" Sermon Delivered August 4, 1889, Metropolitan Tabernacle.

[228] Spurgeon, C. H. "The Unrivaled Friend." Sermon delivered November 7, 1869, Metropolitan Tabernacle.

[229] Spurgeon, C. H. "My Times Are in Thy Hand." Sermon delivered May 17, 1891, Metropolitan Tabernacle.

[230] Spurgeon, C. H. *Eccentric Preachers.* (London: Passmore & Alabaster, 1879), 12.

[231] Spurgeon, Susannah. *Words of Cheer and Comfort for Sick and Sorrowful Souls!* 1898.

[232] Spurgeon, C. H. *The Treasury of David: Psalms 27–57* (Vol. 2). (London; Edinburgh; New York: Marshall Brothers, n.d.), 5.

[233] Ibid., 62.

[234] Ibid.

[235] https://quotefancy.com/charles-h-spurgeon-quotes, accessed November 28, 2022.

[236] *Insight for Today*. "Criticism," July 28, 2022. https://insight.org/resources/daily-devotional/individual/criticism2, accessed November 26, 2022.

[237] Drummond, Lewis A. "The Secrets of Spurgeon's Preaching." https://img.sermonindex.net/modules/newbb/viewtopic_pdf.php?topic_id=13555&forum=34, accessed December 1, 2022.

238 Christie, Vance. "Charles Spurgeon & Christlike Responses to Critics," May 8, 2014. https://vancechristie.com/2014/05/08/christ-like-responses-critics/, accessed October 20, 2022.
239 Ritzema, Elliot, Ed., *Spurgeon Commentary: Galatians.* (Lexham Press, 2013). Taken from the Introduction.
240 Thielicke, Helmut. *Encounter with Spurgeon,* (trans. John W. Doberstein). (Cambridge: James Clarke & Co., 1964), 40–41.
241 Lee, Robert G., "By Christ Compelled" in the *Robert G. Lee Sermonic Library.* (Christ for the World Publishers, Orlando, FL, 1981), 32.
242 Spurgeon, *Lectures to My Students,* 332.
243 Ibid., 326.
244 Ravenhill, Leonard. "Suffering—The Marks of God's Approval."
245 Quoted by Curtis C. Thomas, *Practical Wisdom for Pastors.* (Crossway Books, 2001), 138.
246 https://www.azquotes.com/quote/570772, accessed October 5, 2022.
247 Spurgeon, C. H. "Faith's Sure Foundation," Delivered August 18,1878, Metropolitan Tabernacle.
248 Spurgeon, C. H. *C. H. Spurgeon's Autobiography, Compiled from His Diary, Letters, and Records, by His Wife and His Private Secretary, 1834–1854.* (Cincinnati; Chicago; St. Louis: Curts & Jennings, 1898), 10.
249 Spurgeon, *Lectures to My Students,* 330.
250 Ibid., 333.
251 Ibid., 332.
252 Ibid., 327.
253 Ibid., 332.
254 Spurgeon, C. H. "Away with Fear." Sermon delivered April 9, 1870, Metropolitan Tabernacle.
255 Spurgeon, *Lectures to My Students,* 157.
256 Ibid.
257 Ibid.
258 Clarence Sexton. C. H. SPURGEON FINDS A FAITHFUL FRIEND, August 5, 2014. https://clarencesexton.com/2014/08/c-h-spurgeon-finds-a-faithful-friend/, accessed December 9, 2022.
259 Spurgeon, C. H. "Christ's Loneliness and Ours." Sermon delivered at the Metropolitan Tabernacle, published August 8, 1907.
260 Spurgeon, *Morning and Evening*, April 14 (Morning).
261 Ibid.

[262] Spurgeon, C. H. "Unprofitable Servants." Sermon delivered June 6, 1880, Metropolitan Tabernacle.

[263] *The Sheffield and Rotherham Independent*, April 28, 1855.

[264] Spurgeon, C. H. "Dare to Be Daniel." Sermon published January 15, 1893, Metropolitan Tabernacle.

[265] Beecher, Henry Ward. *Life Thoughts*. (1858), 165.

[266] Spurgeon, C. H. *Lectures to My Students: Addresses Delivered to the Students of the Pastors' College, Metropolitan Tabernacle. Second Series.* (Vol. 2). (New York: Robert Carter and Brothers, 1889), 241.

[267] Spurgeon, C. H. "Tearful Sowing and Joyful Reaping." Sermon delivered April 25, 1869, Metropolitan Tabernacle.

[268] Tozer, A. W. *The Root of the Righteous.* (Chicago: Moody Press, 1986), 165.

[269] Chuck Swindoll. *Insight for Today.* "God at Work," February 21, 2016.

[270] Spurgeon, C. H. "The Still Small Voice." Sermon delivered July 9, 1882, Metropolitan Tabernacle.

[271] Spurgeon, C. H. "A Homily for Humble Folks." Sermon delivered April 27, 1890, Metropolitan Tabernacle.

[272] Spurgeon, C. H. "My Times Are in Thy Hand." Sermon Delivered May 17, 1891, Metropolitan Tabernacle.

[273] Murray, Iain. *Letters of Charles Haddon Spurgeon.* (The Banner of Truth Trust, 1992], 166.

[274] Nettles, Tom. *Living by Revealed Truth: The Life and Pastoral Theology of Charles Haddon Spurgeon.* (Ross-shire, Scotland: Christian Focus Publications, 2013).

[275] https://www.azquotes.com/quote/875722, accessed October 24, 2022.

[276] Spurgeon, C. H. "Ziklag—or David Encouraging Himself in God," Sermon Delivered June 26, 1881, Metropolitan Tabernacle.

[277] Ibid.

[278] Ibid.

[279] Swindoll, Chuck. *Insight for Today. A Daily Devotional* (Pain), August 2, 2017.

[280] Keller, Tim. *Walking with God through Pain and Suffering.* (New York: Riverhead Books, 2015), 30.

[281] Spurgeon, C. H. *Spurgeon's Sermons,* Vol. 17: 1871. (Woodstock, Ontario, Canada: Devoted Publishing, 2017), 200.

[282] Spurgeon. *The Sword and Trowel,* May 1876, 197.

[283] Spurgeon, C. H. "Cheer Up, My Comrades!" Sermon delivered January 1, 1880, Metropolitan Tabernacle.

[284] Himes, Andrew. *The Sword of the Lord: The Roots of Fundamentalism in an American Family.* (Seattle, Washington: Chiara Press, 2011), 291.

[285] Spurgeon, C. H. "Cheer Up, My Comrades!" Sermon delivered January 1, 1880, Metropolitan Tabernacle.

[286] Spurgeon, C. H. "For the Sick and Afflicted." Delivered January 22, 1876, Metropolitan Tabernacle.

[287] Spurgeon, *Morning and Evening*, November 30 (Evening).

[288] Spurgeon, C. H. "Grand Glorying," Sermon Delivered July 5, 1868, Metropolitan Tabernacle.

[289] Spurgeon, C. H. "Lovely, but Lacking." Sermon delivered at Metropolitan Tabernacle, published December 26, 1912.

[290] Spurgeon, C. H. "A Word for the Persecuted." Sermon delivered August 16, 1874, Metropolitan Tabernacle.

[291] George, Christian. *The Lost Sermons of C. H. Spurgeon, Volume I: His Earliest Outlines and Sermons Between 1851 and 1854.* (Nashville: B&H Academic, 2017), Preface.

[292] https://www.thefreedictionary.com/vociferator.

[293] "Mr. Spurgeon's Sermons Burned by American Slaveowners." The Southern Reporter and Daily Commercial Courier (April 10, 1860). See also *The Morning Advertiser* (April 2, 1860).

[294] Spurgeon and the Metropolitan Tabernacle. https://www.elephantandcastle.org.uk/a-brief-history/metropolitan-tabernacle/, accessed January 9, 2023.

[295] Kulp, George. *The Making of a Preacher:* Chapter 9: "The Preacher's Difficulties."

[296] https://www.rylequotes.org/quotes/laughter-ridicule-opposition-and-persecution, accessed February 27, 2021.

[297] Spurgeon, C. H. *The Treasury of David: Psalms 27–57* (Vol. 2). (London; Edinburgh; New York: Marshall Brothers, n.d.), 62.

[298] Spurgeon, C. H. "A Word for the Persecuted." Sermon delivered August 16, 1874, Metropolitan Tabernacle.

[299] Spurgeon, C. H. "The Scales of Judgment." Sermon preached June 12, 1859, New Park Street Chapel.

[300] C. H. Spurgeon. "The Cause and Cure of a Wounded Spirit," April 16th, 1885. http://www.ccel.org, accessed December 8, 2013.

[301] From Spurgeon's letter to Mr. Near, February 22, 1890, Spurgeon's College.

[302] Fullerton, *C. H. Spurgeon,* 313–14.

[303] Spurgeon, C. H. "Forgetting God," Sermon Delivered September 9, 1876, Metropolitan Tabernacle.

[304] Spurgeon, *Lectures to My Students,* 161–162.

[305] Plumer, W. S. *Studies in the Book of Psalms: Being a Critical and Expository Commentary, with Doctrinal and Practical Remarks on the Entire Psalter.* (Philadelphia; Edinburgh: J. B. Lippincott Company; A & C Black, 1872), 581.

[306] Maclaren, Alexander. *The Book of Psalms:* Book II, 164.

[307] Spurgeon. *The Treasury of David,* Psalm 55:12.

[308] Spurgeon, C. H. "Dare to Be a Daniel." Sermon published January 15, 1893.

[309] Spurgeon, C. H. "A Sacred Solo." Sermon (#1423) delivered in 1878, Metropolitan Tabernacle.

[310] Henry, M. *Matthew Henry's Commentary on the Whole Bible: Complete and Unabridged in One Volume.* (Peabody: Hendrickson, 1994), 1000.

[311] http://www.goodreads.com/quotes/tag/betrayal, accessed July 6, 2014.

[312] Rogers, Adrian. "The Root of Bitterness" (article). http://www.oneplace.com/ministries/love-worth-finding/read/articles/root-of-bitterness-8599.html, accessed July 2, 2014.

[313] Jim Henry. Bitterness: Weeding Out the Poisonous Root (sermon). http://www.kt70.com/~jamesjpn/articles/Bitterness.htm, accessed July 3, 2014.

[314] Lucado, Max. *In the Eye of the Storm and Applause of Heaven,* (Two classics in one volume), Chapter 11.

[315] Spurgeon. *Faith's Checkbook,* April 8.

[316] Flood, Charles. *Lee: The Last Years.* (Mariner Books; 1st Mariner Books Ed. Edition, September 2, 1998), 136.

[317] Spurgeon, C. H. "The Christian's Heaviness and Rejoicing." Sermon delivered November 7, 1858, New Park Street Chapel.

[318] Amundsen, Darrel. "The Anguish and Agonies of Charles Spurgeon," in: *Christian History,* Issue 29, Volume X, No. 1, 23.

[319] Ibid.

[320] Ray, Charles. "The Life of Susannah Spurgeon," in *Morning Devotions by Susannah Spurgeon: Free Grace and Dying Love.* (Edinburgh: Banner of Truth, 2006), 166.

[321] W. Williams. *Personal Reminiscences of Charles Haddon Spurgeon*. (London: The Religious Tract Society, 1895), 46.

[322] Spurgeon, *Morning and Evening*, April 12 (Morning).

[323] Ibid.

[324] Spurgeon, C. H. "Unparalleled Suffering," Sermon delivered March 4, 1883, Metropolitan Tabernacle.

[325] Spurgeon, Susannah. *Words of Cheer and Comfort for Sick and Sorrowful Souls!,* Chapter: "In the Darkness Without Jesus," 1898. (Written after the death of her beloved husband, Charles Spurgeon).

[326] Spurgeon, C. H. "Fear Not." Sermon delivered October 4 1857 at the Music Hall, Royal Surrey Gardens.

[327] Spurgeon, C. H. "The Upper Hand." In *The Metropolitan Tabernacle Pulpit Sermons* (Vol. 15, Sermon #901. (London: Passmore & Alabaster, 1869), 637.

[328] Spurgeon, C. H. "The Christian's Heaviness and Rejoicing." Sermon delivered November 7, 1858, New Park Street Chapel. Words in quotation marks summarize Spurgeon's remarks on not knowing why he often broke out crying.

[329] Amundsen, Darrel. "The Anguish and Agonies of Charles Spurgeon," in *Christian History,* Issue 29, Volume X, No. 1, 24.

[330] 11 Reasons Spurgeon Was Depressed, (Staff), July 11, 2017. https://www.spurgeon.org/resource-library/blog-entries/11-reasons-spurgeon-was-depressed/, accessed November 10, 2022.

[331] Spurgeon, C. H. "Nathaniel; or the Ready Believer and His Reward." Sermon delivered April 29, 1888, Metropolitan Tabernacle.

[332] Spurgeon, C. H. "Sweet Stimulants for the Fainting Soul." Sermon delivered December 16, 1860, New Park Street Chapel.

[333] Spurgeon, C. H. "The Valley of the Shadow of Death." Sermon delivered August 12, 1880, Metropolitan Tabernacle.

[334] Spurgeon, C. H. "Israel's God and God's Israel." Sermon delivered March 29, 1868, Metropolitan Tabernacle.

[335] Spurgeon, C. H. "The Saddest Cry of the Cross." Sermon delivered January 7, 1877, Metropolitan Tabernacle.

[336] Spurgeon, C. H. "The Frail Leaf." Sermon delivered at the Metropolitan Tabernacle. Published on Thursday, September 28, 1911.

[337] Spurgeon, C. H. "The Shadow of a Great Rock," Sermon Delivered July 18, 1869, Metropolitan Tabernacle.

[338] Spurgeon, C. H. "The Sinner's Only Alternative." Sermon Delivered December 27, 1861, Metropolitan Tabernacle.

[339] "Spurgeon Can Help Your Depression," November 9, 2017.

[340] Spurgeon, C. H. *Lectures to My Students, Addresses Delivered to the Students of the Pastors' College, Metropolitan Tabernacle,* (Vol. 1). (New York: Robert Carter and Brothers, 1889), 167.

[341] Spurgeon, *Lectures to My Students,* 156.

[342] Spurgeon, C. H. "The Exaltation of Christ." Sermon delivered November 2, 1856, New Park Street Chapel.

[343] Spurgeon, C. H. "The Saddest Cry from the Cross," Sermon Delivered January 7, 1877, Metropolitan Tabernacle.

[344] Hughes, Kent. *2 Corinthians: Power in Weakness,* 30–31.

[345] *The Anguish and Agonies of Charles Spurgeon,* 24.

[346] Spurgeon, C. H. "For the Troubled." Sermon delivered January 12, 1873, Metropolitan Tabernacle.

[347] Spurgeon, C. H. *The Sword and Trowel.* (London: Passmore & Alabaster), 36.

[348] Spurgeon, Charles. *The Complete Works of C. H. Spurgeon, Volume 35: Sermons 2062–2120.* (Delmarva Publications, Inc., 2015), 332.

[349] https://www.azquotes.com/quote/565241, accessed November 30, 2022.

[350] Spurgeon, C. H. "Medicine for the Distracted." Sermon delivered June 8, 1873, Metropolitan Tabernacle.

[351] Spurgeon, Charles. "Joy and Peace in Believing." Sermon delivered May 20, 1866, Metropolitan Tabernacle.

[352] Spurgeon, C. H. "The Christian's Heaviness and Rejoicing." Sermon delivered November 7, 1858, New Park Street Chapel.

[353] Spurgeon. *Lectures to My Students,* 158.

[354] Letter to the *Daily Telegraph* (September 23, 1874), cited in Lewis A. Drummond. *Spurgeon: Prince of Preachers*. (Grand Rapids: Kregel, 1992), 506.

[355] "Spurgeon's Love of Fine Cigars." http://www.romans45.org/spurgeon/misc/cigars.htm, accessed January 16, 2023.

[356] Spurgeon, *Lectures to My Students,* 155.

[357] Ibid., 156.

[358] Spurgeon, *Morning and Evening*, April 12 (Morning).

[359] Spurgeon, C. H. "The Cause and Cure of a Wounded Spirit." Sermon delivered April 16, 1885, Metropolitan Tabernacle.

[360] Spurgeon, *Lectures to My Students,* 164–165.

[361] Spurgeon, C. H. *Flashes of Thought; 1000 Choice Extracts from the Works of C. H. Spurgeon.* (London: Passmore & Alabaster, 1874), Entry #916.

[362] MacArthur, J., Jr. (Ed.). *The MacArthur Study Bible* (electronic ed.). (Nashville, TN: Word Pub., 1997), 1662.

[363] Henry, M. *Matthew Henry's Commentary on the Whole Bible: Complete and Unabridged in One Volume.* (Peabody: Hendrickson, 1994), 2133.

[364] Exell, Joseph S. *The Biblical Illustrator,* (Book of Acts, Vol. 15). (Grand Rapids: Baker Book House, undated), 450.

[365] Exell, Joseph S. *The Biblical Illustrator,* (Book of Acts): *Or Anecdotes, Similes, Emblems, Illustrations; Expository, Scientific, Geographical, Historical, and Homiletic, Gathered from a Wide Range of Home and Foreign Literature, on the Verses of the Bible.* (Oak Harbor, WA: Logos Research Systems, Inc., 1997), 448.

[366] Henry, M. *Matthew Henry's Commentary on the Whole Bible: Complete and Unabridged in One Volume.* (Peabody: Hendrickson, 1994), 2133.

[367] Anonymous.

[368] Exell, J. S. (1997). The Biblical illustrator (Acts): Or anecdotes, similes, emblems, illustrations; expository, scientific, geographical, historical, and homiletic, gathered from a wide range of home and foreign literature, on the verses of the Bible (p. 452). Oak Harbor, WA: Logos Research Systems, Inc.

[369] Spurgeon. *The Full Harvest,* 498.

[370] Ibid., 69.

[371] Ibid., 75.

[372] Ibid., 70.

[373] Chang, Geoff. "The Thermopylae of Christendom": Spurgeon the Pastor and Preaching, August 22, 2022. https://www.spurgeon.org/resource-library/blog-entries/the-thermopylae-of-christendom-spurgeon-the-pastor-and-preaching/, accessed December 29, 2022.

[374] Spurgeon, C. H. "Kept from Iniquity." Sermon Delivered September 22, 1887, Metropolitan Tabernacle.

[375] Spurgeon, C. H. *Autobiography* (Volume 2): *The Full Harvest 1860-1892.*

[376] *Chaplain Magazine.* https://bible.org/illustration/charles-spurgeon-1, accessed December 1, 2022. Note: This is the only source of documentation that I found for the story.

[377] "Spurgeon and the Downgrade Controversy," October 4, 2015. https://jasonkallen.com/2015/12/spurgeon-and-the-downgrade-controversy/, accessed October 19, 2022.

[378] Spurgeon, C. H. *C. H. Spurgeon's Autobiography, Compiled from His Diary, Letters, and Records, by His Wife and His Private Secretary, 1834–1854.* (Cincinnati; Chicago; St. Louis: Curts & Jennings, 1898), 49.

[379] Spurgeon, C. H. "Assured Security in Christ." Sermon delivered January 2, 1870, Metropolitan Tabernacle.

[380] Spurgeon, *Lectures to My Students,* 214.

[381] MacArthur, J., Jr. (Ed.). *The MacArthur Study Bible* (electronic ed.). (Nashville, TN: Word Pub., 1997), 1731.

[382] Henry, M. *Matthew Henry's Commentary on the Whole Bible: Complete and Unabridged in One Volume.* (Peabody: Hendrickson, 1994), 2247.

[383] Spurgeon, C. H. "The Infallibility of Scripture." Sermon delivered March 11, 1888, Metropolitan Tabernacle.

[384] http://christian-quotes.ochristian.com/Charles-Spurgeon-Quotes/page-30.shtml, accessed October 24, 2022.

[385] Spurgeon, C. H. *C. H. Spurgeon's Autobiography, Compiled from His Diary, Letters, and Records, by His Wife and His Private Secretary, 1834–1854,* vol. 2. (Cincinnati; Chicago; St. Louis: Curts & Jennings, 1898), 354–355.

[386] Spurgeon, C. H. "A Sermon of Personal Testimony." Delivered March 11, 1883, Metropolitan Tabernacle.

[387] Spurgeon, C. H. "Scourge for Slumbering Souls." Sermon delivered November 3, 1861, Metropolitan Tabernacle.

[388] Spurgeon. *Autobiography,* Vol. 1, 371.

[389] Ibid.

[390] Exell, J. S. *The Biblical Illustrator: Second Corinthians.* (New York; Chicago; Toronto: Fleming H. Revell Company, n.d.), 132.

[391] Spurgeon, *Lectures to My Students,* 154.

[392] Spurgeon, C. H. *C. H. Spurgeon's Autobiography, Compiled from His Diary, Letters, and Records, by His Wife and His Private Secretary, 1834–1854,* vol. 1. (Cincinnati; Chicago; St. Louis: Curts & Jennings, 1898), 180.

[393] Spurgeon, C. H. *Autobiography* (Vol. 2), 192.

Endnotes

[394] *Sword and the Trowel,* February 1869 notes the six-step process for church membership.

[395] Fullerton, W. Y. *Charles H. Spurgeon, Biography,* Chapter 10.

[396] Spurgeon. *An All-Around Ministry.* (Carlisle, PA: Banner of Truth Trust, 1978), 177. Note: In 1865 Spurgeon founded an Annual Conference of the Pastors' College for all its graduates. Spurgeon gave twenty-seven Presidential Addresses at the Conference; twelve of them compose the book "An All Round Ministry."

[397] Spurgeon, C. H. "Labouring and Not Fainting," Sermon Delivered September 8, 1872, Metropolitan Tabernacle.

[398] Spurgeon. *An All-Around Ministry.* (Carlisle, PA: Banner of Truth Trust, 1978), 177.

[399] Dallimore, Arnold. *Spurgeon.* (Chicago: Moody Press, 1984), 173.

[400] Spurgeon, C. H. Letter to his congregation and friends from Clapham, Tuesday Evening, October 26, 1858. It is cited at the preface to the sermon "God's Barriers Against Man's Sin."

[401] Spurgeon, C. H. "Gospel Missions," Sermon delivered April 27, 1856, New Park Street Chapel.

[402] Spurgeon, C. H. "For the Sick and Afflicted," Delivered January 22, 1876, Metropolitan Tabernacle.

[403] Ibid.

[404] Spurgeon, *Lectures to My Students,* 217.

[405] Spurgeon, C. H. "Suffering and Reigning with Jesus," Sermon delivered January 3, 1864, Metropolitan Tabernacle.

[406] Spurgeon, C. H. "Our Gifts, and How to Use Them," Sermon delivered in 1872, Metropolitan Tabernacle.

[407] Spurgeon, C. H. "Rest, Rest." Sermon delivered January 8, 1871, Metropolitan Tabernacle.

[408] Ibid.

[409] Spurgeon. *Letter, An Exposition of Matthew*, 274.

[410] "Letters of C. H. Spurgeon. http://www.godrules.net/library/spurgeon/NEW2spurgeon13.htm, accessed January 17, 2023.

[411] Spurgeon. *Letter, An Exposition of Matthew*, 274.

[412] From Spurgeon's letter to Mr. Near, February 21, 1888, Spurgeon's College.

[413] Spurgeon, *Lectures to My Students,* 164.

[414] Spurgeon, C. H. "The Unrivaled Friend," Sermon Delivered November 7, 1869, Metropolitan Tabernacle.

[415] Spurgeon, C. H. "A Faithful Friend," Sermon delivered March 8, 1857, New Park Street Chapel.

[416] Ibid.

[417] Spurgeon, *Lectures to My Students,* 164.

[418] Spurgeon, C. H. "A Faithful Friend," Sermon delivered March 8, 1857, New Park Street Chapel.

[419] Spurgeon, C. H. "The Unrivalled Friend," Sermon delivered November 7, 1869, Metropolitan Tabernacle.

[420] Spurgeon, C. H. "A Faithful Friend," Sermon delivered March 8, 1857, New Park Street Chapel.

[421] Ibid.

[422] Williams, W. *Personal Reminiscences of Charles Haddon Spurgeon.* (London: The Religious Tract Society, 1895), 12.

[423] Spurgeon, C. H. "My Times Are in Thy Hands," Sermon delivered May 17, 1891, Metropolitan Tabernacle.

[424] George, Christian T. "Charles Spurgeon's Dangerous Mission," June 19, 2017. https://www.challies.com/sponsored/charles-spurgeons-dangerous-mission/, accessed October 10, 2022.

[425] Sauer, Christof. "To Flee or Not to Flee: Responses to Persecution and the Issue of Relocation." *Missionalia* (Online) vol.41 n.1 Pretoria, Aug. 2013.

[426] Spurgeon, C. H. "My Times Are in Thy Hand," Sermon Delivered May 17, 1891, Metropolitan Tabernacle.

[427] Spurgeon, C. H. "Gratitude for Deliverance from the Grave," Sermon delivered January 3, 1892, Metropolitan Tabernacle. The date must be the time of its revision by Spurgeon, not when actually delivered.

[428] Spurgeon, C. H. "Timely Reflections," Sermon delivered December 27, 1868, Metropolitan Tabernacle.

[429] Spurgeon, C. H. *Autobiography,* 426.

[430] Spurgeon, C. H. "Paul the Ready," Sermon Delivered May 22, 1890, Metropolitan Tabernacle.

[431] Cited in Spurgeon's sermon "A Bottle in the Smoke," delivered March 23, 1856, New Park Street Chapel.

[432] Spurgeon, C. H. "The Christian's Heaviness and Rejoicing," Sermon delivered November 7, 1858, New Park Street Chapel.

[433] Spurgeon, C. H. "Cheering Words and Solemn Warnings," Sermon delivered January 13, 1887, Metropolitan Tabernacle.

[434] Spurgeon, C. H. "Songs in the Night," Sermon delivered at New Park Street Chapel. Intended for reading February 28, 1898, Metropolitan Tabernacle.

[435] Spurgeon, *Lectures to My Students,* 164.

[436] Spurgeon, C. H. "Daniel's Band," Sermon delivered August 3, 1890, Metropolitan Tabernacle.

[437] Henry, Matthew. *Matthew Henry Concise Commentary on the Bible,* (1 Corinthians 12: 1–11).
mhc.biblecommenter.com/1_corinthians/12.htm, accessed December 6, 2011.

[438] Stott, John. *Between Two Worlds,* 320.

[439] Spurgeon, C. H. *Lectures to My Students: Addresses Delivered to the Students of the Pastors' College, Metropolitan Tabernacle. Second Series.* (Vol. 2). (New York: Robert Carter and Brothers, 1889), 57.

[440] Day, Richard. *The Shadow of the Brim*, 156.

[441] Spurgeon, C. H. "Pride and Humility," Sermon delivered August 17, 1856, New Park Street Chapel.

[442] "The Problem with Pride," www.oneplace.com accessed November 27, 2022.

[443] Spurgeon, C. H. "Preach the Gospel," Sermon Delivered August 5, 1855, New Park Street Chapel.

[444] Spurgeon, *Morning and Evening*, November 4 (Morning).

[445] Spurgeon, *Lectures to My Students,* 164.

[446] Spurgeon, Susannah and William Harrald. *Autobiography Diary, Letters, and Records,* Vol. 1, 156.

[447] Spurgeon. *Letter to a friend, Autobiography* 2:100.

[448] Ibid.

[449] Spurgeon, C. H. "The First Beatitude," Sermon Delivered at the Metropolitan Tabernacle, 1873. (Published August 5, 1909).

[450] Spurgeon, *Morning and Evening*, March 6 (Evening).

[451] Spurgeon, C. H. "God's People in the Furnace," Sermon delivered August 12, 1855, New Park Street Chapel.

[452] "Whitefield and the Devil" in J.B. Wakeley, Anecdotes of the Rev. George Whitefield (London: Hodder and Stoughton, 1872), 137–138.

[453] Bonar, Horatius. *Looking to the Cross,* Preface, 1851.

[454] Spurgeon. *An All-Round Ministry,* 303.

[455] Spurgeon. *Lectures to My Students,* Vol. 2, 19.

[456] Spurgeon, C. H. "None But Jesus" (Second Part). Sermon delivered February 17, 1861, New Park Street Chapel.

[457] Spurgeon, C. H. "Micah's Message for Today." Sermon Delivered August 22, 1889, Metropolitan Tabernacle.

[458] Stott, John. *The Message of Galatians.* (Downes Grove, IL: InterVarsity Press, 1968), 179.

[459] Spurgeon, C. H. (1871). New Uses for Old Trophies. In The Metropolitan Tabernacle Pulpit Sermons (Vol. 17, pp. 50–51). London: Passmore & Alabaster.

[460] Packer, J. I. *Rediscovering Holiness: Know the Fullness of Life with God.* (Grand Rapids: Baker Books, 2009).

[461] Spurgeon. *The Full Harvest,* 278.

[462] Spurgeon, C. H. "The Eternal Name," Sermon delivered May 27, 1855, New Park Street Chapel.

[463] Spurgeon. *The Full Harvest,* 505.

[464] Spurgeon, C. H. "What the Stones Say, or Sermons in Stones," Lecture delivered October, 1870, 28.

[465] Carlile, J. C. *C. H. Spurgeon: An Interpretative Biography.* (London: The Religious Tract Society and The Kingsgate Press, 1934), 266.

[466] Spurgeon, C. H. "What the Stones Say, or Sermons in Stones," Lecture delivered October, 1870, 4–5.

[467] Spurgeon, Susannah and William Harrald. *Autobiography Diary, Letters, and Records,* Vol. 1, 4.

[468] Pierson, A. T. *From the Pulpit to the Palm-branch.* (New York: Armstrong & Son, 1892), 22.

[469] Spurgeon, *Morning and Evening*, March 6 (Evening).

[470] *Day by Day with D. L. Moody.*

[471] Hayden, Eric W. "Charles H. Spurgeon: A Gallery of Famous Friends." https://www.christianitytoday.com/history/issues/issue-29/charles-h-spurgeon-gallery-of-famous-friends.html, accessed December 9, 2022.

[472] Spurgeon, C. H. "Glorifying in the Lord," Sermon delivered January 1, 1874, Metropolitan Tabernacle.

[473] Spurgeon, *Morning and Evening*, April 5 (Evening).

[474] Spurgeon, C. H. "Filling the Empty Vessels," Sermon delivered September 17, 1882, Metropolitan Tabernacle.

[475] *Faith's Checkbook,* November 15.

[476] Hatcher, William. *Along the Trail of the Friendly Years.* (London & Edinburgh: Fleming H. Revell Company, 1910), 249.

[477] Spurgeon, *Lectures to My Students.* (London: Passmore & Alabaster, 1883), iv.

478 Spurgeon, Susannah and William Harrald. *Autobiography Diary, Letters, and Records,* Vol. 1, 272.

479 Spurgeon, C. H. "Filling the Empty Vessels," Sermon delivered September 17, 1882, Metropolitan Tabernacle.

480 Taylor, J. Hudson. "Faith in God's Faithfulness." http://articles.ochristian.com/article9560.shtml, accessed December 28, 2022.

481 https://gracequotes.org/quote/depend-on-it-gods-work-done-in-gods-way-will-never-lack-gods-supply/, accessed December 28, 2022.

482 Spurgeon, C. H. "My Times Are in Thy Hand," Sermon delivered May 17, 1891, Metropolitan Tabernacle.

483 Spurgeon, *Morning and Evening*, March 4 (Morning).

484 Spurgeon, C. H. *Lectures to My Students: Addresses Delivered to the Students of the Pastors' College, Metropolitan Tabernacle. Second Series.* (Vol. 2). (New York: Robert Carter and Brothers, 1889), 245–246.

485 White, B. R. *The Baptist Quarterly.* "Charles Haddon Spurgeon: Educationalist. Part 2: The Principles and Practice of the Pastors' College," 87. https://biblicalstudies.org.uk/pdf/bq/32-2_073.pdf, accessed January 8, 2023.

486 Spurgeon, C. H. "The Cause and Cure of a Wounded Spirit," April 16th, 1885. http://www.ccel.org, accessed September 14, 2014.

487 Keller, Timothy. "The Wounded Spirit: Proverbs Series." http://verticallivingministries.com/2014/01/08/tim-keller-on-the-wounded-spirit-proverbs-series, accessed March 12, 2015.

488 Spurgeon, C. H. "The Cause and Cure of a Wounded Spirit," Sermon delivered April 16, 1885, Metropolitan Tabernacle.

489 Ibid.

490 Spurgeon, C. H. "Healing for the Wounded," Sermon delivered November 11, 1855, New Park Street Chapel.

491 Spurgeon, C. H. "The Cause and Cure of a Wounded Spirit." (Sermon # 2494, April 16, 1895). http://www.biblebb.com/files/spurgeon/2494.htm, accessed September 15, 2014.

492 Spurgeon, C. H. *Faith's Checkbook,* May 14.

493 Spurgeon, *Lectures to My Students,* 161.

494 Spurgeon, C. H. "Tearful Sowing and Joyful Reaping," Sermon delivered April 25, 1869, Metropolitan Tabernacle.

495 Spurgeon, Charles H. *Lectures to My Students.* (London: Marshall, Morgan & Scott, 1969), 156.

[496] Spurgeon, Charles H. *Lectures to My Students.* (London: Marshall, Morgan & Scott, 1969), 161–162.

[497] Spurgeon, *Morning and Evening*, August 24 (Evening).

[498] Poirier, Alfred. *The Peacemaking Pastor.* (Baker Publishing Group, Kindle Edition), 9.

[499] Spurgeon, C. H. "Cheer up, My Comrades!" Sermon delivered January 1, 1880, Metropolitan Tabernacle.

[500] Spurgeon, C. H. "The King's Weighings." Sermon delivered August 26, 1883, Metropolitan Tabernacle.

[501] Spurgeon. *An All Round Ministry,* 214.

[502] Spurgeon, *Lectures to My Students,* 163.

[503] Spurgeon, *Morning and Evening*, February 20 (Morning).

[504] Ibid., November 4 (Morning).

[505] Spurgeon, C. H. "Beauty for Ashes," Sermon published January 9, 1913. Delivered at the Metropolitan Tabernacle.

[506] Spurgeon, C. H. "A Jealous God," Sermon delivered May 29, 1863, Metropolitan Tabernacle.

[507] Chappell, Clovis. *Sermons on Biblical Characters.* (New York and London: Harper & Brothers Publishers, 1922), 25.

[508] Wiersbe, Warren. *Be Free* (Colorado Springs: David C. Cook, 1975), 145.

[509] Swindoll, Charles R. *Come Before Winter...and Share My Hope.* (Portland: Multnomah, 1985), 187.

[510] Wilde, Oscar. Quoted in *Sir Arthur Conan Doyle, Memories and Adventures.* (Boston: Little, Brown, and Co., 1924), 73. The same story, with different wording, is also included in Hesketh Pearson. *The Life of Oscar Wilde.* (Middlesex, Australia: Penguin, 1919), 148. The wording here matches Doyle's version, not Pearson's. Cited by Alistair Begg, "Jealousy," (July 28, 2002).

[511] https://www.christianquotes.info/quotes-by-topic/quotes-about-jealousy/, accessed January 5, 2023.

[512] Spurgeon, C. H. "To Lovers of Jesus: An Example," Sermon delivered April 12, 1885, Metropolitan Tabernacle.

[513] Spurgeon, C. H. "Burden Bearing," Sermon delivered August 26, 1886, Metropolitan Tabernacle.

[514] Spurgeon, C. H. "Communion with Christ and His People," Sermon delivered December, 1882, at a Communion service in Mentone.

[515] Tarbell, Martha. *Tarbell's Teacher's Guide to the International Sunday School for 1912.* (New York: Fleming H. Revell Company, 1911), 440.

[516] https://www.moodypublishers.com/authors/m/f-b-meyer/, accessed January 24, 2024.

[517] Ibid.

[518] Spurgeon. *Faith's Checkbook,* May 6.

[519] Spurgeon, C. H. "Rest," Sermon delivered April 18, 1869, Metropolitan Tabernacle.

[520] Spurgeon, C. H. "The Best Strengthening Medicine," Sermon No. 2209 delivered at the Metropolitan Tabernacle and intended for reading June 21, 1891.

[521] Stott John. *The Preacher's Portrait: Five New Testament Word Studies.* (Grand Rapids: William B. Eerdmans Publishing Company, 2017), 98.

[522] *Royal Insignia.* Compiled by Edwin & Lillian Harvey. (Shoals, Indiana: Old Path Tracts Society, 1992), 142.

[523] *Gill's Exposition of the Entire Bible,* 2 Corinthians 12:10.

[524] Harris, M. J. *The Second Epistle to the Corinthians: A Commentary on the Greek Text.* (Grand Rapids, MI; Milton Keynes, UK: W.B. Eerdmans Pub. Co.; Paternoster Press, 2005), 866.

[525] Spurgeon, *Morning and Evening*, November 4 (Morning).

[526] Spurgeon. *An All Round Ministry.* (Carlisle, PA: Banner of Truth Trust, 1978), 328.

[527] Spurgeon. *The Full Harvest,* 398.

[528] Spurgeon. *An All Round Ministry.* (Carlisle, PA: Banner of Truth Trust, 1978), 208.

[529] Ibid.

[530] Ibid.

[531] Ibid., 220.

[532] Spurgeon, C. H. "God's Cure for Man's Weakness," Sermon delivered June 24, 1866, Metropolitan Tabernacle.

[533] Exell, J. S. *The Biblical Illustrator: Second Corinthians.* (New York; Chicago; Toronto: Fleming H. Revell Company, n.d.), 495.

[534] Spurgeon, C. H. "The Best Strengthening Medicine," Sermon No. 2209 delivered at the Metropolitan Tabernacle and intended for reading June 21, 1891.

[535] Spurgeon, C. H. "God's Cure for Man's Weakness," Sermon delivered June 24, 1866, Metropolitan Tabernacle.

[536] Spurgeon. *The Full Harvest,* 310–330.

[537] Spurgeon, C. H. "Morning and Evening Songs," Sermon delivered in 1873, Metropolitan Tabernacle.

[538] Spurgeon, C. H. *Autobiography* (Vol. 2), 192.

[539] Wright, William. *The Wit and Wisdom of Rev. Charles H. Spurgeon.* (Baltimore: R. H. Woodward Company, 1894), 7. Note: Wright cites it was 13 acres, while Charles Ray says it was 9 in his book *Charles Haddon Spurgeon*, 415.)

[540] Spurgeon, C. H. *C. H. Spurgeon's Autobiography, Compiled from His Diary, Letters, and Records, by His Wife and His Private Secretary, 1834–1854,* vol. 2. (Cincinnati; Chicago; St. Louis: Curts & Jennings, 1898), 356.